PRAISE FO

"*I think, for a rapidly evolving business world,* UpSolutions *may be as significant to business owners today as* The E-Myth *was thirty years ago. It helps create a critical mind shift essential for greater profitability and sustainability for any business.*"

—**Dan Benamoz, Pharmacy Development Services**

"UpSolutions *puts business owners in the driver's seat with strategies for differentiating themselves from their competition and for turning their team members into heroes for their customers.*"

—**Dan Sullivan, Founder and President, *The Strategic Coach®, Inc.***

"*Easy or hard? The two ways to grow a successful small business! Patti Mara has encapsulated all of the critical pieces necessary to do it the easy way. Trust what your clients are telling you, let your team help design the solutions your clients need, and above all else design your delivery to add value to your clients' decisions. They will be loyal! This is a must-read primer for all small business owners! We know it works—we thrived while training with her and continue to this day!*"

—**Len Hume and Annette Marchionda, Owners, PCS of Niagara**

"In this articulate and engaging book, Patti Mara shows you how to capitalize on strengths you're currently overlooking to better serve your customers, increase your margins, and permanently escape competition. Her UpSolutions process is easy to understand and implement and is based on years of experience working with business owners and teams. If you'd rather provide solutions than sell, and would rather build relationships than simply handle transactions, then this book is for you. I highly recommend it!"

—**Shannon Waller, Strategic Coach**

UPSOLUTIONS

UPSOLUTIONS

TURNING TEAMS INTO **HEROES**
AND CUSTOMERS INTO **RAVING FANS**

PATTI MARA

Copyright © 2020 by Patti Mara.

All rights reserved. No part of this book may be used or reproduced in any manner whatsoever without prior written consent of the author, except as provided by the United States of America copyright law.

Published by Advantage, Charleston, South Carolina.

Printed in the United States of America.

10 9 8 7 6 5 4 3 2 1

ISBN: 978-1-94963-945-2
LCCN: 2019918994

Cover design by Carly Blake.
Layout design by David Taylor.

This publication is designed to provide accurate and authoritative information in regard to the subject matter covered. It is sold with the understanding that the publisher is not engaged in rendering legal, accounting, or other professional services. If legal advice or other expert assistance is required, the services of a competent professional person should be sought.

This book is dedicated to my many mentors and teachers, with a special thank you to my parents, who demonstrated the importance of relationships.

AS YOU READ THROUGH THIS BOOK AND APPLY THE CONCEPTS TO YOUR BUSINESS AND TEAM, THERE ARE ADDITIONAL RESOURCES, TOOLS, AND VIDEOS ON WWW.UPSOLUTIONSBOOK.COM.

TO YOUR SUCCESS!

CONTENTS

INTRODUCTION 1

CHAPTER ONE 11
THE OPPORTUNITY IN CHANGE

CHAPTER TWO 25
UNDERSTANDING YOUR CUSTOMERS

CHAPTER THREE 45
THE WISDOM AND EXPERIENCE IN YOUR BUSINESS

CHAPTER FOUR 57
UPSOLUTIONS: THE RECIPE

CHAPTER FIVE 71
HEARING THE MESSAGE, NOT JUST THE WORDS

CHAPTER SIX 93
TOTAL CUSTOMER FOCUS AND EXPERIENCE

CHAPTER SEVEN 109
TEAM ENGAGEMENT AND TRAINING

CHAPTER EIGHT 127
THE NEED FOR CONTINUOUS EVOLUTION

CONCLUSION. 141
BRAVE NEW WORLD

ABOUT THE AUTHOR 149

ACKNOWLEDGMENTS 151

INTRODUCTION

"Are you playing the right game of business?"

We are living in a period of rapid change. Independent businesses are trying to adapt and struggling to compete in the global economy. What so many of these companies are learning, however, is that you can't break new ground with an old business model.

Most people think their business is what they sell, their products and services. What they don't realize is that when they compete with other sellers on price, they are giving away their wisdom and expertise for free. Competing on price means that your business is being commoditized. Playing Walmart and Amazon's game is the wrong approach for your unique independent business. The good news is that the chains and big-box stores—any transaction-based seller—can't play *your* game, the business you already excel at: being a valued resource for individual customers, building relationships with them, and providing *solutions* rather than selling one-size-fits-all products.

This book will show you how to shift your business from being commoditized to the value of the solutions you provide and the relationships you cultivate. You will know you're playing the right game of business when your team members become brand ambassadors for the company and heroes to your customers. The result: your customers are raving fans who sing your praises and send more customers your way.

Every day, I am inspired by independent business owners who succeed and thrive by playing their own game of business. The entrepreneurs who thwart the competitive pressures of chains, global internet sales, and price-driven markets are innovators in their fields—heroes, even. They are the business leaders to learn from. This book will share the success strategies that make them great, the strategies that form the core of my business—which is to help them reach even greater heights.

One of my favorite examples of a business turnaround is Chris Cornelison, a pharmacy owner in Iuka, Mississippi, population around three thousand.

Chris had a dilemma: he knew that customers picking up their prescriptions didn't always know about the side effects that came with them. Chris wanted people to know that probiotics offset the gastrointestinal woes caused by antibiotics, and that statins to lower cholesterol deplete the coenzyme Q10, which is necessary for cells to produce energy. Chris knew that taking COQ10 would relieve the muscle aches that patients on statins experienced.

When he tried to sell those products along with the medications, however, he couldn't seem to get any footing in the marketplace. And his employees were not thrilled about becoming a sales force.

What could he do to better care for those patients and get his team's buy-in?

"I was attacking it from the product," Chris says. "But when we started thinking about *the problem we were trying to solve* instead of *the product we were trying to sell,* it completely changed our mind-set."

That pivotal shift also increased his sales from double to triple

INTRODUCTION

digits, brought his store rave reviews—which in turn brought in new customers—and encouraged him to launch his proprietary brand of problem-solving supplements, SolutionsRx, which is now sold in more than two hundred independent pharmacies in the US.

Chris coined the term for this problem-solving approach UpSolutions. And when I heard the term, it was a perfect fit for the approach I've used with clients. With his permission, I now use it. (Thanks, Chris!)

UpSolutions is a simple strategy to expand your business success by increasing your value to customers. First, as Chris did, you identify a customer's problem. Then you educate the customer about the problem—say, an antibiotic's side effects—and explain how you can fix it. Then you explain why that is the *best* solution.

That simple recipe is how you turn customers into raving fans and your team into heroes. It also brings teams together, because whether you're the company president or a cashier at the counter, everyone wants to be part of positive outcomes.

The UpSolution recipe is a core component of my Profit Generator Program—Turning Your Customer Experience into Profit. I've worked with hundreds of entrepreneurial owned and operated businesses to reposition their business for success. By focusing on the inherent value you already deliver—for instance, helping customers make buying decisions they're happy with—you can achieve measurable results in terms of greater profits; team engagement, productivity and retention; customer loyalty; and strategic positioning in the marketplace.

> The value in your business is not your product or service, it is *what you do* to sell your product or service.

The value in your business is not your product or service, it is *what you do* to sell your product or service. It is what differentiates you. It is the value you bring to the market by responding to your customers' needs and wants. Seeing your company from your customers' perspective raises your awareness of their problems and pivots you toward solving them. Any business can find its shifting point—the value-add that propels you to better results. Every business can identify what its customers need and, just like Chris, discover that a shift in thinking will create significantly better results.

They can make that shift by listening to their customers first rather than reacting to industry experts and pundits, market predictions, and competitors' prices. When Walmart started offering $4 prescriptions, for instance, a local drugstore like Chris Cornelison's cannot hope to compete solely on price. The challenge is Walmart creates the impression they are the lowest price by advertising $4 prescriptions. What's missing in the ads are that it will take hours to fill (so you shop their store and spend more money!), that there are limited medications offered at $4 (and the other medications will cost you a lot more), and they cannot offer the same level of service and personalized attention with a pharmacist. So, while a chain creates a *perception* of lower prices with one or a few discounted items, they profit by sales of many additional products.

While pricing is a component of business strategy, independent stores can't position solely by lower their pricing to compete with the chains—and they shouldn't. That is playing the wrong game—your competitors' game. This isn't to say that pricing strategy shouldn't play a part in your game. For instance, pharmacist Dave Marley, the owner of Marley Drug in Winston-Salem, North Carolina, turned the challenge of competing with Walmart $4 prescriptions into an opportunity and launched an extended supply generic drug program, which discounts drugs bought in three-month or six-month quantities. His innovative program offers customers a solution to their medication costs while providing Marley Drug's personalized support for its customers' long-term needs.

Playing the right business game means identifying what puts your company in the unique position to solve your customers' problems. Today, Chris Cornelison sees every customer walking through his door as an opportunity to care for someone by solving a problem. So does every member of his team. Chain stores can't play *his* game of business.

> Playing the right business game means identifying what puts your company in the unique position to solve your customers' problems.

I've been fortunate—and delighted—to see firsthand how many independent businesses have boosted their market value by listening closely to their customers to identify and solve problems. There was the motorcycle store owner whose helmet sales were being commoditized even though custom-fitted helmets would keep riders safer, maybe even save their lives. When he branded his store's fitting process and offered customers coupons to buy their helmets from him at a special price, his business grew, and so did customer loyalty.

A friend of mine is an avid skier. She was in Station Ski & Ride in Markham, ON, getting her skis tuned and waxed when Holly asked about a heated ski boot display (Holly hates cold feet!). While she was looking at the heated boots someone else came in and asked if they had any Black Friday specials. The team's response was they don't have sales because when you purchase from them you are paying for their expertise in fitting your equipment. It was a two-hour process to have Holly's new heated boots fitted (Holly says they are fantastic!).

Shortly after, someone Holly knew bought her ski boots at a Canadian sporting good chain. They took the newly purchased boots into Station Ski & Ride to have them fitted and it turns out she had purchased boots two sizes too big for her! The value in getting the right boots the first time.

Every one of these companies offered a compelling reason for customers to choose *them*. And it was never the lowest price—it was the *solution* they created for their customers' problems.

Customers are the gold mine for every independently owned and operated business. I saw this truth for the first time in 1987, when I was supporting myself through college by working in a mall bookstore. It was a chain bookstore, so we could have rung up one purchase after another and never gotten to know the shoppers who streamed in from the mall. But the store manager's greatest strength was training her employees in customer service. When customers walked through the door, we would stop whatever we were doing to welcome them and ask if there was anything we could help them find. If they were looking for a specific book, we'd take them to the section where it was located and put the book in their hands. If we didn't have it in the store, we'd offer other book suggestions or check if we could order it. (We were a small store, so we weren't supposed to do that, but thanks to the manager, we custom-ordered all the time.)

It was incredible how often a customer would come back in and say, "I just want to say thank you. I've been to almost every store in this mall, and this is the only one where I felt welcome and appreciated."

That little store was targeted to do $500,000 gross revenue that year. Instead, we did just over $1 million.

A big factor in this tremendous team achievement was how engaged everyone working there was. We had a lot of *fun* working with one another and interacting with customers. And the results spoke for themselves.

INTRODUCTION

Everything I talk about in this book started from that work experience. Seeing the happy—and bottom-line—results of mindful and genuinely helpful customer care put me on the path to where I am today. I learned, just as Chris Cornelison learned, that employees love being part of positive outcomes. They don't want to sell products, and customers don't want to feel sold. But when you can see your customer react with pleasure—and often surprise, because they're not used to a business going the extra mile for them—it transforms the work experience. Engagement and enthusiasm transform people who didn't want to be in sales into your best salespeople.

Shifting your business focus from transactions to customer relationships is the difference between upselling and UpSolutions. Upselling is trying to sell more by asking, "Would you like fries with your burger?" That automatic question to everyone is designed to encourage a bigger transaction-based sale.

UpSolutions repositions independent businesses to cater to their customers' specific needs. These companies are already creating value in their marketplace or they wouldn't be in business—but they may be struggling. Many independent businesses feel squeezed right now. Most of those companies are at a transition point because the way they have done business in the past has stopped working for them.

Think about your business twenty years ago, or even ten. Markets were more local, less global. All you had to do was unlock the door to your store and people would come in. Today's entrepreneurs must look closely at who is coming in that door if they want to thrive in the present and plan for the future. No longer will even your most loyal customer wait two weeks for a part to come in. Not with Amazon Prime promising to get it to them within two days.

Throughout history, businesses that found shifting points and pivoted have succeeded, and the ones that protested, "But we've always done it this way!" are gone. Are you old enough to remember when milk was delivered in glass bottles directly to your doorstep each morning? (If you aren't, yes, there really was such a time!) Up to a certain point, the crowning innovation of that business was swapping a horse and cart for a truck. But then the world changed again. Packaging changed. Refrigeration improved. It was cheaper to consolidate delivery to stores. No longer cost-efficient, the old ways became unprofitable. Dairy farmers and distributors needed a paradigm shift. Customers were no longer willing to pay more for delivery.

That's just one example of a business that went through a pivotal shift—and you know what happened, since there are no more milk trucks stopping at every house in town.

But your business can also make a pivotal shift. In fact, it will make multiple shifts over time. Family-owned companies know this—each generation creates new ways to connect with its customers.

So many independent businesses are feeling squeezed right now—by chain stores, online shopping, extra working hours, lower profit margins, and their inability to compete on price. But these are the businesses that create the richness in their markets, and they are the backbone of every community. When they are strategically positioned and their teams are trained to focus on solutions for customers, the national and multinational businesses can't touch them.

UpSolutions guide companies to see their market advantage with their customers. Awareness is key. I call it "educated observation." When you offer solutions based on feedback from your customers, you have unlimited

> **When you offer solutions based on feedback from your customers, you have unlimited opportunity for growth.**

opportunity for growth.

But how do you get there? How do you refocus employees from tasks to results? How should you train new team members? How do you create an environment in which everybody succeeds? Business owners need the weight of their teams behind them. Every employee is valuable—and can be more so.

When an industry paradigm shifts, how do you shift with it? How do solutions spring from awareness? How do they become a core value of your independent business? And when do you shift and pivot again?

In the following chapters you'll find the answers—UpSolutions—for independent businesses. These are my strategies for seizing the unlimited opportunity that's already at your fingertips. My goal is to turn your team into brand ambassadors for your business and heroes to your customers, and to turn your customers into raving fans.

I will show you how to:

- understand how to define your business by solutions, not product or service sales;

- create your own marketplace by clearly differentiating what you do;

- engage your employees with tools to make a difference;

- add to your value for customers through your relationships with them;

- create raving fans by going beyond service to solutions;

- focus on the value your business already has (that you may be taking for granted);

- maintain your customer focus through "educated observation"; and

- see significant improvements in profits, customer engagement and loyalty, and team buy-in and retention.

Throughout my career I've been blessed with phenomenal teachers and mentors, many of them my own clients. I've come to love working with entrepreneurial businesses because everyone on the team is on the court. Everyone's efforts contribute to the company's results. Everyone makes a difference. Everyone matters. The companies that believe this and live this are the ones that have the greatest impact on their customers and communities.

It takes a tremendous amount of courage and heart to be an entrepreneur. When you recognize the gold mine that is your customer base, you already have the basis for your success. Now you just have to clearly define your market advantage—every independent business has one. Your product or service is the vehicle to create value for your customer, not the value itself!

Every independent business has the opportunity for boosting its success and creating brand ambassadors, heroes, and raving fans.

It's been a privilege and a joy for me to watch my entrepreneurial clients transform their companies with UpSolutions.

Are you ready to apply UpSolutions to your business?

CHAPTER ONE

THE OPPORTUNITY IN CHANGE

No independent business owners or team members like change when it feels imposed on them. It's one thing to choose to reinvent your business because you want to. It's quite another to feel compelled to change because you're struggling to stay alive. For everyone on the team—all the way from owner to clerk—change is stressful, sometimes bumpy, and always uncertain.

And yet change we must. As business continues to undergo tectonic shifts driven by technology, the resources upon which our whole economy is based will be reallocated. As entrepreneur, engineer, and author Peter H. Diamandis writes in his book, *Abundance: The Future Is Better Than You Think,* "Technology is a resource-liberating mechanism. It can make the once scarce the now abundant."[1]

What Diamandis has noticed is that in a global marketplace, every time our resources dwindle to the point of scarcity, emerging

---

[1] Peter H. Diamandis, *Abundance: The Future Is Better Than You Think* (New York: Free Press/Simon & Schuster, 2012).

technology shifts us into abundance again. Up until recently, our whole model has been based on an economy of scarcity, supply, and demand. In today's economy, when we experience scarcity, money to invest in technology becomes available. Tech development brings us back to abundance.

He uses the oil and gas industry as an example. When we perceived these resources as scarce, technology offered three new paths: create access to more oil; use the energy we have more efficiently; and develop alternative fuels. We shifted our focus. This is the paradigm for every industry. As Diamandis writes, "One of the better responses to the threat of scarcity is not to try to slice our pie thinner—rather it's to figure out how to make more pies."[2]

His examples include information, made abundant by search engines such as Google; energy, through wind and air; and communications, through mobile networks. YouTube creates an abundance of entertainment, and technology-driven transportation (electric cars, self-driving vehicles) is burgeoning.[3]

All this spells opportunity for entrepreneurs. If your business is struggling (scarcity), investing in resources for your growth puts you on the path to prosperity (abundance). The wonderful thing is that you already have the resources you need—the UpSolutions recipe for generating business success shifts your focus to what your secret sauce is.

There is an incredible opportunity in the change that *your* industry is undergoing now. (I can say "your industry" with confidence because *every* industry is undergoing change at what seems like ever-increasing speed.) Opportunity is the upside of change; when we welcome change, we embrace opportunity. Opportunity

---

2   Ibid.

3   Ibid.

is playing the right game of your unique business, not struggling to play the commodity game that chains play, which is focused on the lowest price.

There are many real-world examples of how opportunity can be found in change.

Online booking and travel planning, for example, made the traditional commission-based business model for travel agents unsustainable. As their backend commissions fell to $0 overnight, many agents left the industry. They weren't used to charging their customers, and their customers weren't used to paying them. Their services were devalued. Travel agents needed a new business model that showcased why choose them. They had to think about their business differently. They had to be able to offer services that customers would be willing to pay for.

The travel agents who stayed and thrived were the ones who were able to show their unique value to clients—value that went far beyond discounted booking sites and price bidding.

One travel agent in Toronto answered that challenge by leveraging his love of diving. Based on his own knowledge and experience, he created specialty scuba trips. He was able to recommend dive shops, the best destinations, safe diving locales, and the best times of year to dive there. He created dive experiences that amateur enthusiasts simply couldn't get on their own or with the help of unfamiliar online providers. His clients felt safe and confident on their dives and had truly unique experiences.

An older couple, both travel agents, enjoyed cruises when they took their own vacations. When self-booking changed the travel business, they realized they had a lifetime of experience on the sea that they could draw upon to maintain their value. They used their knowledge as cruise mavens to plan unique and customized cruises especially for seniors like themselves. With aggregate pricing, they could focus on the customer experience—an experience they were intimately familiar with. Their clients knew the cruise would be suited to *them*.

One of my favorite local food markets, Goodness Me, found an opportunity in the crowded field of grocery and organic foods. Everything about the store is inviting, from its design to the quality of its meat and produce and natural healing remedies. What sets Goodness Me apart from other natural food stores, however, is the seminar room, which is equipped with a full kitchen. There, healing practitioners hold workshops as well as a signature ten-week "Life Watchers" course on nutrition and wellness, using products that are available in the store. At the end of those ten weeks, you're a raving fan of Goodness Me—and you're also healthier. Yes, these markets charge higher prices, but I am happy to pay them because I feel good about what I'm buying.

Big chains own the grocery business, and many independent owners feel squeezed, which is why it's easier to find a Safeway than a Goodness Me. But the chains aren't driven by what propels the owners of Goodness Me, Janet and Scott Jacks, a husband and wife team who learned about sourcing and eating natural foods in order to manage Scott's type 1 diabetes. Goodness Me plays a different game than the big chains play because of its owners' commitment to health and wellness. And, by embracing technology, the couple added even more value with a vibrant online store. Janet has written a book, *Discover the Power of Food*. She also blogs and has a podcast, all focused on helping people make healthy choices.

We've already seen how Chris Cornelison discovered his right business game when he catered to his pharmacy customers' problems by using his knowledge of solutions. When you solve your customers' *challenges*, the value you provide is immeasurable. I think a lot of independently owned businesses could be described as labors of love. Their value lies in the insight, experience, and enthusiasm of their owners and teams.

For instance, in the era of Amazon-everything, there is an independent bookstore that provides value way beyond overnight shipping to its patrons. Queen Books owners Alex Snider and Liz Burns were passionate readers who made their bookstore space a home for communities of other passionate readers. They offer classes, book clubs, and discussion groups for readers of all ages. If you love to read, you have a home there.

> When you solve your customers' *challenges*, the value you provide is immeasurable.

All these entrepreneurs found opportunity in the changes they were confronting by clearly defining their value to customers.

Chain stores advertise the lowest price to bring customers in, and then count on those customers spending more time and money in the store. PBS's Frontline did an interesting expose on Walmart's business model (available to watch online) titled "Is Wal-Mart Good for America?" One of Walmart's strategies is to advertise the lowest prices (Walmart's Rollback). For example, advertising a $25 microwave. Good price if you were thinking about buying a new microwave! However very few people buy the $25 model (minimal features) and instead buy a $50 or $60 one assuming because $25 is the lowest price they are still paying the lowest price for the model they choose. And usually you can find the same higher priced microwave somewhere else for less money.

Walmart (and other chains) create a perception of being the lowest price on everything in their stores because they constantly advertise low priced items.

Misleading? Possibly. The challenge is a local independently operated business can't compete by out advertising the chains. Instead they need a different way of positioning why choose their business.

YOUR EXISTING VALUE

When price competition threatens to commoditize you as an independent owner—when you feel forced to match a competitor's pricing—it is easy to miss the real value of your business to customers. That value is already present in your existing business—it just may not be immediately obvious.

Take the case of the motorcycle store owner in Northern Ontario, dealing with online competition selling helmets at reduced prices. One response would have been to reduce the price of his helmets, which would cut heavily into his margin. He couldn't afford to be commoditized, and his was not a commodities-based business at heart. (And what's at heart is important in terms of realizing your value to the customer.)

This store owner told me something interesting. With everything he sold, he was especially passionate about properly fitting helmets to individual riders because that helmet could literally one day save the rider's life. He said that most people are riding around with poorly fitted helmets; in some cases, they've picked their helmets out because the helmet matches their bike, not their head. He knew that custom-fitted helmets would keep riders safer, and even save their lives.

In fact, his shop was so committed to helmet safety through custom fitting that it already had its own measuring and fitting process. He wasn't just selling helmets, he was offering the value of proper helmet choice, fit and protection. But like many other independent store owners, he was finding that even when customers came in to check out his store—and get fitted for a helmet—they would leave and then buy the helmet online for $25 to $50 less.

I suggested that he name and brand his custom helmet-fitting process. Then charge customers $50 to be properly fitted with a helmet (and position why the proper fit was so important) and offer the rider a $50 coupon for purchasing a helmet at their store.

He did just that. He branded his fitting process with a coupon to offset the cost of the fitting to helmet buyers in his store. His business grew, and so did customer loyalty. His customers felt safe with him.

THE NEW RULES OF BUSINESS

As the stories above show, independent businesses are vulnerable to price-squeezing commoditization if they don't shift their business model from sales to solutions. (And creativity will flourish as a result!) With the changing marketplace there are new business rules.

First, if you are competing on price—you are focusing on sales. The opportunity is to change your focus to solutions (New Business Rule #1: Shift from Sales to Solutions).

Second, we are shifting away from a business model based on transactions to one based on relationships. If you haven't made that shift, you're being commoditized

> if you are not clearly communicating why customers should choose your business—what your value is to them—then people will choose the perceived lowest price.

(New Business Rule #2: Shifting from Transactions to Relationships).

And finally, If you are not clearly communicating why customers should choose your business—what your value is to them—then people will choose the perceived lowest price, which is the game the Chains play—creating a perception of being the lowest price (New Business Rule #3: If you don't clearly communicate why choose you, people choose the lowest perceived price).

Let's take those rules one at a time.

SUCCESSFUL INDEPENDENT BUSINESSES SHIFT FROM SALES TO SOLUTIONS

If you are still focused on the product in your interactions with customers, you are missing an opportunity, not just in making the sale, but in building customer confidence and long-term loyalty. For instance, if you sell TVs, are you telling someone about a TV set or are you finding out what type of programming the customer likes to watch? Sports? News? Animation? Action? What is the size of the room the TV will be in? A buyer's needs inform the purchase, from screen size to remote functions to smart device connections. If you can find out the buyer's needs by asking specific questions and then based on their identified needs make a TV recommendation (and explain why) now you are creating a solution and the customer will walk away with the best option for them and happy with the purchase decision.

When you focus on solutions, people are willing to pay for perceived value. If you create a unique solution for them, you have created perceived value. Think of the motorcycle shop's custom-fitted helmets.

SHIFTING FROM TRANSACTIONS TO RELATIONSHIPS WITH YOUR CUSTOMERS

Sales and transactions metrics overlook two key factors: who your customers are and what their lifetime sales potential could be. Customer engagement is vital—it's the difference between upselling and UpSolutions. It's moving away from the mind-set of "Do you want fries with that?" to "What do you enjoy eating?" Building relationships with individual customers is a total team effort; for employers, that means training. Your team members need to know that their job is to engage customers before they ever ring up a sale on the cash register. When it comes to shifting from transactions to relationships, everyone is important. Who wants to shop in a store where no one looks up?

CLEARLY COMMUNICATE YOUR VALUE, OR CUSTOMERS WILL CHOOSE THE PERCEIVED LOWEST PRICE

Customers choose the lowest *advertised* price, which creates a perception of lowest price. That may not really be the case; when a business model is based on lowest advertised price, it gets people into the store, where they may then spend more money for upgraded products or more products.

An independent business can't match the advertising spend that a national or international chain store employs—it's just not feasible. Your job is to clearly communicate why choose your business—what value do you offer your customers they won't get anywhere else. The challenge for most business owners (and their teams) is that we tend to take for granted the value we provide in order to sell our products and services.

Often the value is showcased in how you guide your customers to make an effective buying decision.

YOUR MOST VALUABLE ASSET: YOUR CUSTOMERS

These new business rules speak to the internet's impact, both on sourcing and distribution. The marketplace is now global—you can get anything from anywhere in the world without leaving home. The internet has shifted the game for *all* businesses, but "local" businesses have a built-in asset not found in cyberspace: actual people to interact with. Even if your independent business is online, you still need to have a relationship with your customers.

It is also why your existing business and customers are your most valuable assets. Think of the wisdom and experience that you and your team have amassed. And in your customers, you have potential lifetime loyalists. These are your two best advantages: your existing customers, who pay you for the value you deliver; and the wisdom in your business that inspires the solutions you provide based on your customers' needs.

Every business has these two advantages. If you have customers who have already bought from you, then you know you are offering something that people want. You want to begin making that pivotal shift from a transactional focus to a relationship focus by determining who your best customers are, and what they need from you, and then offering it to them. The reward is increased revenue per customer, increased customer retention, and increased repeat business—all of which means increased profit.

Your team members gain experience and knowledge of the business every day from working with customers. The problem for many businesses (and people) is that they take what they know for granted. It's human nature to think, however unconsciously, that we all think the same way and know all the same things. We don't. There are always opportunities for learning.

> Your customers often don't even know the questions to ask to make an effective decision.

Whatever your business is, at a very basic level you transform a complex issue to a simplified solution for your customer. People buy products and services for a reason—what is it they are trying to accomplish? When you become genuinely curious about your customers and focus on the solutions you can offer to their needs, you will have an unlimited opportunity for growth. There is always the next solution you can offer—applying your wisdom and experience to your target audiences needs.

This requires a mindset shift, and awareness that your customers often don't even know the questions to ask to make an effective decision. Understanding this key point allows for a very different customer engagement which is all about solving their needs.

But it's not enough to learn how to fulfill their wants and needs. You must also clearly communicate *why* they should choose your business by highlighting the value they will receive from your company. If you don't clearly convey that, you are destined to compete on the default factor: pricing. Local businesses have the power to change the commodities business model to a model of their choosing; that's playing the right game of business—your game. The seeds of your future success are in your current business! Take nothing for granted—everything you see and hear from customers is data you can use to refine how you communicate your value.

When a business takes its value for granted, so do its customers.

However, when you can see your business from your customer's perspective, you achieve what a friend of mine calls "20/20 insight." For instance, what's not working for customers in their experience of your business? How can you use that data to change a practice or reposition your company? Why do they patronize your business now? How can you leverage their appreciation so that you can continue growing together?

The way to weather change is to embrace the opportunity in its winds. There is *always* a new direction to go in. Lamenting change gets you nowhere—and dates you to "back in the day." I can't stress this enough: *today* is the day! No business has to close or be sold because "it's not what it used to be." If you look for *what else it could be*, you are bound to find opportunity.

Embracing the opportunity in the change means throwing out some long-established measurements of success. For instance, in the commodity economy, growth for a company used to mean getting bigger, literally. Today, however, growth no longer means expanding your store into the adjacent space left when the pizza parlor moved. Your growth opportunity is more likely to be marked by the community your business creates—like the community created by the Queen Books' book lovers.

SHARING YOUR EXPERTISE

Another approach to finding—or updating—your opportunity is to recognize that customers don't necessarily know how to make informed buying decisions. And they want to. Businesses that do not engage their customers often force them to make "hit and miss" choices. When they guess wrong, they often complain not about their lack of knowledge, but about the store. Independent businesses are in the position to prevent customers from making bad choices, educate customers, and build relationships so they can make smart decisions. Your team members have opportunities to share their expertise every time the door opens. In fact, anyone who's worked in a company for three months knows more about what the customer needs than the customer does!

> Anyone who's worked in a company for three months knows more about what the customer needs than the customer does!

Case in point: a friend of mine who works at a clothing retailer gets this question on almost an hourly basis: "Does this make me look bad?" What the shopper really wants to know is "Do I look good?" An experienced retailer will ask questions: "Are you going to an event? When and where is it? Are you hosting it or are you a guest? Will you be comfortable standing and sitting in that dress?" The people who help customers make effective buying decisions are the ones to whom customers return time and again. The experience and knowledge of your team members makes customers feel heard.

Every team member in every business can be the equivalent of a personal shopper. The opportunity in the change can be as simple as finding a way to help one customer or rearranging your space to make your customers' in-store experience faster and easier.

Identifying opportunity invariably repositions your company. People need to know why they should choose you and not your local or national competitors. You are using opportunity to bring about a mind-shift in your management, your team, and your customers. When you expand your opportunity, you also expand your marketplace.

The first step is identifying your target audience customers and finding out what is important to them, how can you make their life better? How is what you offer a solution to their needs?

And that begins with understanding your customers.

CHAPTER TWO

UNDERSTANDING YOUR CUSTOMERS

Understanding that the heart of your business lies in the value you create for your customers is the first step toward engaging with them consciously, constantly, and profitably. The solutions you provide for them go beyond your list of products and services. Your business is not what you sell, it's the solutions you provide, and your products and services are a vehicle to deliver value. I can't stress enough that pivoting from a transaction-based business to a relationship-based business depends on your understanding of your customers. And not just *your* understanding, but that of your entire team. When you see your business through your customers' perspective, you enhance both your value to them and

> Your business is not what you sell, it's the solutions you provide, and your products and services are a vehicle to deliver value.

their value to you.

Whether you own a tea shop, a spa, or a heating and cooling business, the sale is not about the commodity. Your real business is the *value* you're selling. Value can't be commoditized. Relationships must be cultivated—real relationships, not just friendly hellos.

To know your customers means having a sincere interest in their needs and their well-being. It isn't enough to be friendly. To create value for them, you have to hear and understand what they tell you.

One of the biggest challenges for businesses today is to be able to put themselves into their customers' mind-set. When you do that, though, you will understand why they make buying decisions because you will know what's important to *them*. It takes awareness and practice to cross the divide that separates the business owner's and customers' mind-sets. But this is where your independent business has the strategic advantage over a chain store: your business is already personal to your clientele and your community. You will be building on that sense of connection and community.

UNDERSTANDING THE CUSTOMER

The key to shifting your mind-set from transactions to relationships is putting yourself in your customers' shoes. Understanding who your customers are and what is important to them sets you and your team up to be UpSolutions providers. It also makes working with your customers much more fun—and turns your team members into heroes.

Understanding what is important to your customers gives you unlimited opportunity for growth. If you are struggling to compete, you may be focusing on staying afloat when the real goal is finding the growth opportunity. Let your customers lead you; let them show you how to apply your company's experience to their needs. This understanding leads you to increased profit, increased revenue per customer, increased customer retention, and a reenergized team. This deep understanding is your secret weapon.

I recently went to the locally owned pet food store where I buy my dog and cat food; my cat food supply was running low. I know the owner well, but she wasn't there that Sunday. Instead, there was a new clerk at the counter. She said "hi" and was very nice when I walked in. I went to get my usual brand of food and found only one container. Since I usually buy eight to ten at a time, I went back and asked at the counter, "Do you know if you have any more? Can you check the back?"

The new clerk walked to the freezer (where I had just been), looked on the shelf (where I had just looked), and said, "We only have what's on the shelf."

"We only have what's on the shelf."

That reply is a classic transactional approach to customers—she offered nothing to me, a customer with a problem that needed a solution. This is where you say to a customer with an unmet need, "Let me see when the next order's coming in," or "Let me leave a note for the store owner or manager," or "Can I suggest an alternative until the next shipment comes in?"

I collected the one container and a few other items. I'd brought a bag, but as I checked out, she didn't bag my purchases. She stacked them, and then watched me as I bagged them. My thought was she had probably worked at a local chain grocery store; that's what they do —but now she was working in an independent store where personalized service is the norm. She didn't see the experience from my perspective. She answered my question, and she was very friendly—

asn't *taking care of me*. It was a perfect illustration of the between customer service and *customer care*.

I love the store and have gotten to know the team over the years, so I went back and shared my experience with the owner later. She was receptive and appreciative.

Liz said, "Thank you. She's a recent hire. I will talk to the weekend manager and make sure of two things: first, that she's the right fit for us, and second, that we get her the training she needs so that's not the experience she's creating for customers." (Thank you, Liz!)

> Customer attrition by disappointment is exactly what independent businesses *cannot* afford.

But what if I didn't have a relationship with that store already? I—and most customers in that situation—would just go to another store the next time we needed pet supplies. And customer attrition by disappointment is exactly what independent businesses *cannot* afford.

So, how do business team members, from the owner to the cashier, learn to understand their customers' mind-set? There is a way—let's call it Ten Steps to UpSolutions:

1. Commit to making this process intentional, deliberate, and proactive.

2. Identify your target audiences—who are your best fit customers?

3. Answer the question, "Why do your customers want what you offer?"

4. Understand that making a sale is never the end of that sale.

5. Know your customer acquisition cost.

6. Engage all team members in the process—and change their mind-set.

7. Go beyond what you see.

8. Be the customer.

9. Offer consistent customer experiences.

10. Take a walk around the store—and don't forget to look up.

Let's look at each of these in turn.

COMMIT TO MAKING THIS PROCESS INTENTIONAL, DELIBERATE, AND PROACTIVE

Don't leave your understanding of your customers to what you might overhear by chance! Answering all questions is an absolute must, but initiating interaction with customers is even better. You can make every conversation meaningful, including those with customers who decline your help. They are also providing valuable data on what creates a positive shopping experience for them. They may tell you what they want or need that you don't have, or haven't thought of yet. They may affirm or challenge your idea of who is a "best fit" customer for your business.

The biggest clues about the value you provide naturally come from the customers who best fit your business. So, identify your best-fit customers. Describe them. What makes them the best fit?

And think clearly about how you define your best-fit customers. "Best fit" does not necessarily mean you see them every week, for instance. As someone who personally does not love to shop for clothes, I won't be in my favorite clothing store every weekend. But when I come a couple of times a year, you can bet that I will leave with more than $1,000 worth of merchandise because the employees show me clothes they know I'll like.

"Best" also doesn't mean the customers who have no complaints or issues with you. The way you handle an issue may be the very thing that brings a customer back. Unhappy customers feel heard and understood when you apologize for what they've experienced, offer a solution to fix it, and then let them know that you did.

Your best customers are the ones who know they can rely on you to satisfy them with more than products and services. They ask for and use your advice, they're open to suggestions for alternative solutions, and they are your most enthusiastic boosters—your raving fans. They are the customers who tell their friends about you. They are the customers who take risks on new products or hairstyles or tools based on your recommendation—because they trust you.

Consumer confidence is all about trust—trust built on the framework of a relationship. And when your entire team is trained to understand and be aware of your customers' mind-set, your customers trust your entire team. Training your team on customer engagement is critical to your success, and I will talk more about it later in the book.

It used to be that if you opened the door of a neighborhood shop, the neighborhood found its way inside. But in today's market, even local businesses are touched by global commerce, which has brought competition, wider access to products, new delivery systems, and new privacy and security concerns. If you want to earn your customers' trust in this business environment, you need to know them completely.

This is not only true for bricks-and-mortar businesses. An independent business can be successful online. Amazon doesn't need to be your competitor; it's a fantastic distribution channel that can grow your reach and reputation. (I found a wonderful locally produced organic skin-care product this way.) Your business can build a following of raving fans who found you by using Facebook, Instagram or Google, along with the ones who activate your door chimes.

A great example of a business that nailed understanding its customers is an independent online store that sells baby strollers. The owner would buy year-end inventories from manufacturers and offer better pricing online. Sure, they were left over from the original stock and might not come in this year's color, but they were safe and well made. His deals weren't the chief incentive for purchasers, however. The value he offered was making their decision-making easier. He knew that new parents are overwhelmed and undereducated about strollers and the number of choices they have are confusing. So, he created an online quiz that took the buyer through important purchasing decisions.

For instance, do you want a stroller that accommodates a car seat? How many children do you want to push? Are you planning to run and jog with it? Do you want something lightweight? Where do you plan to use it—sidewalks? Beach? Rough pavement? Trails? He then used customers' answers to make customized product recommendations. His business was an instant hit.

IDENTIFY YOUR TARGET AUDIENCES

Many people are surprised to learn that most businesses have not one target audience, but anywhere from two to five. I haven't come across a business yet that has only one "right fit" customer. Think about the different groupings of people who depend on your business, and the different solutions you provide for them. Do you know who your target audiences are? Do you know what they value?

Your target audiences are the subsets of customers you enjoy working with, who value what you do for them and are willing to pay you for it, even when it means some inconvenience to them. They may travel an extra distance to get to you. Parking may be a hassle, but they come anyway. They may wish you had different hours, but come whenever you're open.

Sometimes businesses have different divisions—with different customer bases that will affect who you sell to and who is on your team. Even if you have a storefront or offer a service, you'll have different target audiences. Example: a pharmacy might primarily serve seniors, people with young children, and college students. Or it might focus on helping patients cope with specific diseases, such as diabetes.

When you analyze who your target audiences are, look at their demographic makeup. What age range are they in? Which economic bracket? What are their interests? That same information could describe about 80 percent of each target audience. You'll also want to ask about areas specific to your business. If you sell furnaces, for instance, you'll want to know how many of your potential customers own their own homes.

To some extent, target audience identification is based on who comes into your business, but understanding those customers allows you to create a strategic marketing message that will ultimately reach a much wider audience. Start with who your best customers are *right now*. If you can identify who they are, what's important to them, and why they choose your business, then you can market your brand to other customers who fit that profile.

When you really connect with your target audiences, they will bring you more of their own business and recommend you to others who need similar solutions. Customer enthusiasm motivates your team, which makes it more fun to work for you, which leads to higher team retention. Your target audiences will always tell you what they need, and this opens up unlimited opportunities for growth.

If your business has more than five target audiences, you may be too scattered to maximize your growth opportunity. Don't be afraid of losing anyone who doesn't fit into a target audience for *your* business; not everyone will. You want the customers who keep coming back and really appreciate the solutions you offer.

A wonderful example of a business that knows its target audiences is a women's retail store in Washington, DC. Its target audiences are affluent women (it's in an affluent neighborhood) age forty-five to ninety-five (there are two assisted living facilities within walking distance) who appreciate unusual clothing (a gem in an otherwise conservative city—nobody would mistake DC for Berkeley); those who need comfortable shoes because they walk a lot or stand for hours in the course of their jobs (e.g., teachers); and high-profile women who dress for special events, give speeches, and appear on television (it's Washington).

The staff at this store is trained to identify and fill specific needs by selecting clothes for time-pressed customers who are uncertain about their look—and occasionally by selecting clothes that will look good on TV.

When you know your target audiences, you will also know who *isn't* likely the best customer fit for your business. You can find ways to create value for them, but without jumping through hoops. Knowing your target audiences makes you more efficient at serving both those who fit and those who don't.

Example: at the clothing store in Washington, customers sometimes bring their teenage daughters in to shop for clothes. The team knows that their clothes do not suit teenagers; a fifteen-year-old girl is not going to come out of there looking cool. To minimize this problem, team members find myriad tactful ways to communicate what they're thinking: "Take her to Target! You'll both be a lot happier!"

Working with pharmacy owners brought home to me the value of knowing your target audience. For example, they might serve young families with children; women going through hormonal changes; seniors with specific geriatric needs; or patients with diabetes and high blood pressure. No store can be all things to all people—which is why a town can have multiple pharmacies, all with different target audiences.

Once you identify yours, you have to communicate to them what makes your business special to *them*.

ANSWER THE QUESTION, "WHY DO YOUR CUSTOMERS WANT WHAT YOU OFFER?"

If you don't know what puts your customers in one of your target audiences, you are probably failing them. It's important to look at your customer retention, and specifically at what brings in repeat business.

In the last chapter I used a little bookstore called Queen Books as an example of how to differentiate a business's value. Why do individual customers choose to purchase books from one seller over another? Amazon seems to dominate the book world, yet some independent bookstores continue to thrive. Why is that?

Because their owners' focus is not on selling books—more often today, it is on creating a community hub for readers. Bookstores are where both local and world-famous authors come to talk and sign their books. They may have a children's section that young readers (and their parents!) love. Bookstores host launch events. Some offer amenities like cafés and comfortable seating where you can literally curl up with a book. This is how Queen Books became beloved in The Beach area of Toronto.

Customers want what Queen Books offers because it supports their love of reading. Comfy seating and pleasant space and lighting encourage you to literally sit and take your time. You don't have to rush. You know which staff-reviewed and recommended books you'll love, because you know and trust the team.

Maybe you know of a bookstore like this in your community. The store takes special orders. It offers member discounts. It hosts book clubs and trivia nights. It's not just selling books! It is selling the connections readers make with books and with other readers. It's selling community.

When you can answer the question, "Why do your customers want what you offer?" you are in the right business game.

UNDERSTAND THAT MAKING A SALE IS NEVER THE END

When you take the approach that a sale is never about the transaction, you begin to see that thriving in business is an *ongoing process* built on relationships with your customers. Over time your customers will change, your team will change, and the solutions you offer will change. Understanding your customers is a key part of a mind-set that stays poised to adapt to changing customer needs. It's always thinking, "What's next?"

At the same time, companies need to maintain continuity through changes in customers' needs. For example, a business called Professional Carpet Solutions (PCS) in St Catherines, Ontario offers an array of carpet cleaning and maintenance solutions to both residential and commercial customers. The commercial end of the business is usually very price-focused—commoditized—and customers who call for price quotes mainly go for the lowest quote.

What PCS owners Len Hume and Annette Marchionda thought to do was examine why different businesses needed clean *surfaces*—not just carpets. The husband and wife team discovered a variety of reasons: companies wanted clean surfaces to maintain their investment in their infrastructure, support the health and well-being of their team, and create a positive impression for their customers. Customers who come into a clean, pleasant environment are more likely to think well of the business and to interact with the team. (Think of how dirty floors distract you as a customer!)

Len and Annette created a zone cleaning system for their commercial accounts. They looked at the high-traffic areas and the less-trafficked areas in companies and then designated zones according to how frequently they needed to be cleaned. They scheduled cleanings based on need. Customers quickly saw the value of a contract with PCS: they had more confidence and peace of mind about maintaining their infrastructure, they believed they were getting a good deal in cleaning certain areas only when necessary, and their team was better organized around the schedule. Had Len and Annette only quoted a price to a prospective customer, they might not have gotten the business. But knowing a sale isn't the end, they asked customers what was needed, and the zone solution was born. Their customers felt a genuine, personal connection with people who understood their business and felt trust and confidence in the relationship over time.

KNOW YOUR CUSTOMER ACQUISITION COST

Retention and repeat business are where companies make their profits, so it is important to know the cost of your customer acquisition—the cost to attract a new customer. Does what you spend on marketing your business pay off in loyal customers?

What's the acquisition cost of a happy customer? If you were to take your entire marketing budget for attracting new customers to your business and then divide it by the number of new customers who come in and stay with you, that's your basic acquisition cost. Companies promote their value through marketing in many ways: advertising (traditional and online), customer loyalty cards, targeted special sales, seminars, food and wine tastings at hospitality businesses, sponsorships, in-store promotions, and endless innovative strategies to bring people in.

You can calculate your customer acquisition cost on a monthly or yearly basis. It's data you need to know to calculate how many times a customer has to do business with you on average before becoming profitable to you. For most independent businesses, it takes an average of three interactions with the same customer—three opportunities for engagement and solutions—before you have paid back the acquisition cost and now generate a profit.

It's an ongoing process too. Even if you're the best in your business at customer service and customer retention, there is always some attrition—customers move away, their circumstances change, they die. The companies that are best at customer retention are the companies that constantly work to attract new business. Independent businesses can't rest on their laurels. Think of the restaurant owner you know who has been in business for thirty years—and just introduced Uber takeout delivery.

ENGAGE ALL TEAM MEMBERS IN THE PROCESS

I will explain this in greater detail in chapter 7, but I want to introduce it here because it is critical to understanding your customers. It makes the difference between, say, a customer buying pet food online or buying it from you.

One reason I always return to my favorite clothing store is that anyone who works there can help me get dressed (figuratively speaking). Obviously, the clothes suit my style, but it's the personal service, which is consistently excellent from every team member, that makes me a raving fan. They understand their customers so well that all I do is go and stand in a dressing room and somebody brings me cool things to try on and helps me figure out which ones I like. They also bring me things I would never have thought to look at if I'd browsed the racks on my own.

When engaged and motivated team members provide solutions to customers, they become invested in the customers' happiness. One retail team member explained to me, "It's so much fun when that happens, because they make you feel like a million bucks, like you were the only clever person in the world who knew this would look good on them."

Independent business owners must understand their customers thoroughly, and the entire team must be *equally* engaged and informed. Often with start-ups, the owner is wholly involved with customers at first. But as the business and the team grow, the founder becomes more removed from the front-line activity—not by choice, but by the panoply of tasks necessary to run the company. I hear this all the time from pharmacy owners. When they went into business, they knew all their customers and went the extra mile to take care of them. Then, when they grew to the point where they couldn't be on the bench all the time and hired other people, it became easy to lose touch, and harder to stay current with their raving fans.

Full team buy-in and alignment is necessary in every business. Your customers' mind-set determines their purchase decisions, so the team's job is first to understand who the customers are and what they need, and then to educate and offer solutions. Keep in mind that customers don't always know the right questions to ask to make effective buying decisions. And it takes a lot of effort for customers to make a buying decision; once they have made a decision, they generally don't want to take the time and effort to revisit it. You want to help people make the decision to choose your business and keep coming back.

Every team member who has worked more than three months in a business knows more about what your customers need than the customers. Each of them should be able and eager to help customers make educated decisions—and create a pleasant and satisfying experience for them.

GO BEYOND WHAT YOU SEE

We all think and reason from our own perspective, our mind-set. Naturally, this means that we sometimes project our thoughts, our knowledge, and our awareness onto other people. It's easy to forget that customers don't know what we know. We take our experience for granted, and we take what we offer for granted. That's why it's easier to focus on *what* we sell, rather than the value we provide.

> We take our experience for granted, and we take what we offer for granted. That's why it's easier to focus on *what* we sell, rather than the value we provide.

A pharmacist, for instance, knows

every medication a patient is taking for the condition or symptom it's designed to treat, the side effects that may occur, and potential interactions with other medications. It would be a disservice to patients for the pharmacist *not* to share what they know about a drug's impact if it's in the patient's best interest.

Educating the customer is key in every business, whether the customer is buying a TV or switching to a vegan diet. To give them the full benefit of your knowledge, you and your team must understand more about your customers than what you see when they come through your door. You must remember what it is you know that the customer doesn't.

BE THE CUSTOMER

The best way to get out of your own mind-set and into your customers' is to *be* a customer! As writer Peter Gurney first pointed out in a 2001 article entitled "A Curious Phenomenon," by virtue of the fact that we're all customers, we all should be experts at customer service, right?[4]

Anyone who has been put on hold longer than it takes to make a three-minute egg, or who has waited in an airport line when a flight has been cancelled, will vouch that this is not the case. It's as though when people cross to the other side of the counter, they forget what the experience of being a customer is like. Independent businesses can't afford to do that.

We have to be able to get into our customers' mind-set. What's important from *their* point of view, not *ours*? Finding that out is a learned skill.

---

4   Peter Gurney, "A Curious Phenomenon," Service Intelligence

Start by thinking of good and bad situations in which you were the customer. What immediately comes to mind? The bad ones, right? The bank where you waited and waited and then the teller closed the service window. Trying to get customer service on the phone when you're stuck in voicemail jail. We've all experienced the unofficial motto of airline customer service: "We're not happy until you're not happy."

Now think of the good experiences you've had as a customer. The store that took back the item even though you'd lost the receipt. The urgent care clinic that stayed open late when your child's fever spiked. The business that went the extra mile for you when you needed help fast.

To be a customer means remembering how hard it is to make a decision when you feel confused or overwhelmed by choices. So many things compete for our attention that we want certainty in unfamiliar places. And we want to feel appreciated. We want to feel cared for.

Here's an example of a missed opportunity from a customer's point of view. A spa is located literally right around the corner from me, and I used to go there regularly. But the owner was so focused on revenue, on pushing product and trying to lock people into time slots, and I got tired of being upsold all the time. The staff wasn't interested in what I wanted or what was important to me. And I was the target market! That spa missed the mark on its own demographic by pushing sales instead of relaxation and rejuvenation. Even though the location is convenient, I now drive to a different town to a different spa.

When I talked to the owner about this, he couldn't seem to escape his mind-set and visit mine. He was polite and open to having the conversation with me, but he just couldn't or wouldn't get into my head. When you can't imagine what it's like to be your own customer, it's a sign that your mind-set is too entrenched. Your best remedy: be the customer.

OFFER CONSISTENT CUSTOMER EXPERIENCES

People often talk about creating "wow" customer experiences, and if you can create an experience that your customers love, that's fantastic. But it's more important to create a *consistent* customer experience.

Here's what I mean: One day, a friend of mine went into his neighborhood dry cleaners, as he did on a regular basis. The owner came out from the back and said, "Mr. Smith, I've got your cleaning right here, sir!" And he went right to his waiting clothes; my friend didn't even have to pull out his ticket. He walked in and was given his suits and left the store feeling valued and pleased. He thought, "Wow, they know me!"

Not two weeks later he went back to the same business and the owner was there again. But this time, he didn't even look at him—he just took the ticket, retrieved my friend's dry cleaning, and rang him up.

"That's strange!" another friend said when she heard the story. But it's not strange; for many customers at countless businesses, that's normal. Because people are mostly focused on what's going on in their lives, they're not *consistently* paying attention to the customer.

When the owner or team members neglect that all-important relationship, depriving customers of a consistent experience, their customers' trust and sense of security falter. They no longer feel as welcome.

In the bookstore where I worked in the eighties, there was a sign on the back of the stockroom door that led to the store. It read,

"Whatever's going on in your life, it's important, but leave it back here. Out there it's all about the customer!" (Feel free to steal that.)

TAKE A WALK AROUND THE STORE— AND DON'T FORGET TO LOOK UP

Another way to understand your customers is to do a walk-through of your business. Role-play as a customer. I recommend doing this once a month, or at least on a regular basis. Do it with different team members so they get used to thinking from the customer's perspective.

You may encounter surprises when you do this. For example, I was once doing a store walk-through with a pharmacy owner, and when I looked up, I saw bunches of wire and screws hanging way up by the ceiling. It turned out that a Christmas decoration had been mounted there, and whoever had taken it down had left the wire up. Nobody on the team, including the owner, had noticed! But customers notice things like that.

When you go to a restaurant and see a dirty awning outside and cobwebs inside, do you want to eat there? We tend to miss those details because we see our business everyday and what the customers see falls into the background of our awareness.

Listening to your customers doesn't just mean verbal give and take. You have to experience your business as *they* experience it. They may be seeing cosmetic flaws you don't notice—and questioning the general quality of your business.

Every customer experience holds insights for your business. When customers perceive something—in your space, in your attentiveness, and especially in your attitude—they build opinions based on it. Make sure that their perspective is positive.

The bottom line for understanding your customers is that independent businesses cannot afford transaction-based interactions. If customers don't feel taken care of, or if they don't feel important, they'll go somewhere else. The antidote to that is understanding exactly who your customers are and what's important to them. When you know that, and consistently offer solutions that show you know it, you have unlimited growth opportunities. If you're listening to your customers, they will always tell you what they need and what they want next.

You must know who your customers are to engage and train your team to use the UpSolutions recipe. This knowledge is the starting point of positioning your business as a solutions partner.

CHAPTER THREE

THE WISDOM AND EXPERIENCE IN YOUR BUSINESS

A key part of providing your customers with value-based solutions and an experience that enhances the value you create is recognizing this simple fact: your customers don't know what your team knows! Once you are clear on who your customers are and what's important to them—your target audiences and their specific needs—the next step is to understand the untapped wisdom you *already* have that is not being applied to solve customer needs.

Your wisdom from experience is the next component that differentiates your business from chains and commodity-based competitors. Think about the gold mine you have: you and your team interact with customers every day, which makes you an expert in quickly spotting what a customer needs. When you use your experience-based knowledge of your customers, you'll see countless opportunities to create value, educate, and offer solutions.

You already know more than you think. If you own an independent business or have worked in one for longer than three months, you know more about your customers than they know about themselves (in the area your business applies to). You just don't know that you know it—yet.

Maybe you take that wisdom for granted because it's what you see and do every day, and you don't stop to think about it. But the fact is that your customers don't know all the ways you can help them. You and your team have solutions for problems they don't even realize they have. When the entire team operates with this awareness, they offer solutions that create positive outcomes for customers, an engaged and enthusiastic team, and an independent business with raving fans.

Applying your wisdom and experience are so valuable. I call this resource applied to your target audiences' needs the core "profit generator" of your business. When you identify target audiences, get clear on who they are and what they need, and then align what you offer with what customers want, you position your business as your customers' solution partner. You can transform the knowledge that you could easily take for granted into a key—even strategic—part of your success.

When you know who your customers are and the value you provide them, you can train your team to be so customer-aware that they will recognize the problem they can solve for the customer even before they say hello. By consistently identifying problems you can solve for customers, you shift your team's mind-set from product to solution.

There are five truths you must understand in order to apply your team's knowledge to growing your business:

1. Every team member is an expert in your business.

2. Every team member can turn wisdom and experience into solutions.

3. Every team member must be fully engaged in the goal of UpSolutions.

4. Every team member helps create your perceived value to customers.

5. Every team member sets the groundwork for UpSolutions with three key mind-set shifts.

EVERY TEAM MEMBER IS AN EXPERT IN YOUR BUSINESS

Think about it: you are subject experts compared to your customers. But we tend to take our accumulated wisdom for granted. We also tend to assume that everyone knows what we know. Because of that, we often make the mistake of not offering or communicating what we can provide. If we think customers are already knowledgeable, we assume we don't have anything to tell them.

It's not just the owner who may assume this; it's the whole team. And it is the whole team that can help customers make effective buying decisions by identifying the problem *and* offering the solution. If you serve customers, your *job* is to educate them and offer solutions. I feel so strongly about this point that I believe if you're not educating and offering, you're ripping your customers off. You are shorting them on your value by not offering what you can do for them. They can't even ask you for your value, because they don't know what's possible—but you do!

The pharmacy business has great examples of the team knowing more than the customer. For instance, when a patient who has been newly diagnosed with diabetes presents their first prescriptions, they may have no clue what those medications do. Maybe they have to be on insulin for the first time in their life and they're terrified. If your pharmacy just fills their script and sends them on their way, you are doing this patient a disservice. But if a team member educates them about when to take it and shows them how, provides the patient with a contact for questions, you've offered them a solution that will bring them back with the next prescription. By spending the time with them, explaining how the drugs work, and answering their questions, you can help enormously in making patients feel confident about their prescribed treatment.

Or let's say a mom comes in with a crying child who has a fever. She may only be there to pick up a prescription, but if she doesn't have a thermometer at home, she'll be going home with a sick child and no way to check her temperature. She'll be forced to bundle the child up again and go back to the pharmacy. The team should anticipate this and ask her if she needs a thermometer—or anything else that would support a child with a fever.

The same principle applies to every business. Start by acknowledging what you as the owner and your team members already know about customers, based on your unique experience and training. This knowledge can help your team identify what you have to offer to customers. Then educate those customers and make the offer, or better yet, give them a choice of offers. For instance, in the pharmacy example, maybe the medication comes in pill or liquid form—one may work faster, while the other works longer but needs to be refrigerated. Which does the customer prefer? Maybe the liquid form comes in flavors for children—we have banana, strawberry, and bubble gum—what's your child's favorite? If the customer chooses the pill form, where will she keep this medication? If it's going to be kept in the child's room, you might recommend a child-proof cap. Sharing your expertise means identifying solutions for customers, educating them about the solutions, and then offering them.

EVERY TEAM MEMBER CAN TURN WISDOM AND EXPERIENCE INTO SOLUTIONS

It's a team effort, and it's the owner's role to educate the team. Team members must be fully equipped, know the advantages of various solutions, and know what questions to ask. Their knowledge will also come from experience. After just three months of interacting with customers—answering their questions, hearing their issues, and learning their needs—patterns emerge. You know what people are looking for. Team members may know more than the owner, especially if the owner has stepped back from the day-to-day operations and now has less contact with customers.

When team members become experts, it's not just customers who benefit; the business does too. Your employees often have great ideas for improvement because they're the front line of your business, day in and day out.

A great example of that came from the Walt Disney Company, where I attended a Disney Institute training in Orlando, Florida. A common customer issue at Walt Disney World was people forgetting where they'd parked—the Magic Kingdom has more than twelve thousand parking spaces, and multiple parking lots can be almost a mile away from the park's entrance and ticket center. The lots are so massive that Disney recommends you take a photo of your space! The park had trams from the parking lot for customers, but they needed a better way than a customer's memory to get people back to their cars.

A tram operator came up with the idea that's now used when guests forget where they've parked. Previously, the driver would announce the stop: "We're in Goofy, Aisle 3." But if the guest didn't remember Goofy or Aisle 3, the solution was to wait until most of the park had cleared out and then drive confused people around until they recognized their cars. Imagine the frustration level of a guest who has been in the park all day with young children. Now it's 10:00 p.m., they're exhausted, they're crying, they're probably having meltdowns. (The children *and* the adults!) Now their last memory of a happy day at Walt Disney World is the &#&%! parking lot.

But the team, who knew the guests best, worked on this, and it was a driver, not management, who figured out the solution. The driver thought, "Instead of going around and telling people a lot name they've forgotten, why don't I keep a log?" Now, when visitors forget where they parked, the drivers ask, "What time did you arrive at the park? Let's take a look at your ticket." They match the entrance time stamped on the ticket to their log so they know where they were when they picked up the guest.

The driver was able to devise this simple solution to a common guest problem because team members are experts at what they do every day. He used his wisdom and experience to change the guest experience at the park.

EVERY TEAM MEMBER MUST BE FULLY ENGAGED IN THE GOAL OF UPSOLUTIONS

The mind-set shift is what distinguishes upselling from UpSolutions. It takes no customer awareness to ask, "Do you want fries with that?" It takes full customer awareness to think, "What does this person actually want or need?" When you are focused on products instead of identifying problems you can solve, your business is commoditized and your team doesn't look up.

Conversely, an engaged team looks for opportunities every day and sees growth ideas for the business. They create a better experience for the customer. They give owners a feedback loop. They feel recognized for their contributions, and as I know from my first bookstore job, they also have more fun! We all felt important in that business, and we continually looked for ways to improve the customer experience.

> An engaged team looks for opportunities every day and sees growth ideas for the business. They create a better experience for the customer.

What stood out for me in my early bookstore job is that team members made the offer, but it was always up to the customer to make the buying decision. The focus on solutions, not sales, is key here. There are no winners in upselling—the team doesn't like selling and customers don't like to be sold. But everyone wants to create value and see the rewards in happy customers.

I can't stress enough that when all team members understand and operate as experts, business improves according to all indicators—customer retention, customer referrals, sales, and profit. You'll see an increase in team retention too. This is important to an independent business because turnover means training new employees, which can mean inconsistent customer experiences.

To increase your team's engagement, you have to treat your team members as if they're your customers. As the owner, your employees are really your first line of customers because the experience you create for them is what they will create for customers. Whatever the owner models will be demonstrated and duplicated, positive or negative. As authors Karl Albrecht and Ron Zemke write in their book, *Service America!*, "If you're not serving the customer, you'd better be serving someone who is."[5]

Team engagement is key to your business—it's the hub of your value delivery system. It creates repeat business, which increases the lifetime value of a customer.

The goal is to raise the whole team's awareness of every customer in the store. For instance, at a clothing and gift store I know, team members are trained to spot customers carrying clothes and immediately ask them, "Can I start a dressing room for you?" Or, "Would you like a hand basket for those little items?" Customer awareness doesn't end until a customer leaves the store. The experience is personal right down to the sale: during the buying process, the counter staffers make eye contact with the customer, compliment what they're buying, and ask how they want the item folded.

They also give the customers answers to questions they haven't asked aloud: "I've removed the security dye tag." "I took the price tag off your gift." "I folded the receipt so the staple won't snag your clothes." And then they thank each customer personally for the sale; if they don't already know the customer's name, they look on her credit card.

There are many ways to tell your customers, "I'm paying attention to you," and the payoffs can be amazing. For example, the

---

5   Karl Albrecht and Ron Zemke, *Service America!* (New York: McGraw-Hill, 2001).

owner of another pharmacy, Chancy Drugs, in Valdosta, Georgia, shared with me that a woman came into one of his stores to pick up an antibiotic. The pharmacist recommended a probiotic and cited research to explain why.

The woman said, "I actually know that, and I've read the research, but I greatly appreciate you saying that, because no one's ever mentioned it to me before." It turned out that she was the human resources manager for a local company with more than seven hundred employees. That exchange led to a relationship with her company that led to Chancy Drugs providing resources and medications to support the health and wellbeing of all of their employees.

Engaged teams show customers that they are *informed* teams. My local cheese shop is known for its variety of unique cheeses. You can sample them and consult with staff members about what to pair them with, knowing you can always trust their recommendations.

EVERY TEAM MEMBER HELPS CREATE YOUR PERCEIVED VALUE TO CUSTOMERS

The focus of training your team to be fully engaged is to be as helpful to your customers as possible. Your value to them is only what they perceive it to be. For instance, a local retailer has trained the team to offer to assist senior citizens and disabled customers who might want help trying on clothes, something that shows the store's value to them. One customer who has multiple sclerosis gratefully accepted the offer one day and now shops there regularly.

When you think about your own best experiences as a customer, invariably they come down to the perceived value provided by a company's helpfulness. For example, everybody has a story about how an airline let them down. Coming home on an international flight last year, I was supposed to change planes in Houston. A thunderstorm delayed my landing, and then my connecting flight was cancelled because of the weather. The airline booked me on the next flight, but didn't tell me! I had to stand in line to find out I'd been rebooked. That flight wasn't until the next day, and then it was delayed for another eight hours. An agent told me, "We may get you home today, or it may be tomorrow." I was left with I'm a number to them and they just don't care.

This would have been a perfect opportunity for the airline to draw on its wisdom and experience from years of rearranging flights for inconvenienced passengers. That airline is now my last choice to go anywhere. An independent business cannot afford to ignore or minimize customer problems and delay solutions. It is critical that you identify the team's accumulated wisdom, consistently apply that knowledge to customers' issues, and offer solutions.

EVERY TEAM MEMBER SETS THE GROUNDWORK FOR UPSOLUTIONS WITH THREE MIND-SET SHIFTS

In the first three chapters of this book, we talk about shifting your business mind-set from transactions to relationships.

The first pivotal mind-set shift is to find the opportunity in whatever it is that's driving change in your business. Opportunity is an unlocked door. It's not necessarily an easy one to get through, but what we choose to do can be the difference between stepping in—and stepping up—rather than bumping against it.

The second mind-set shift is the awareness that your customers are the key component to your success. You do this by identifying your target audiences, knowing them inside and out, and creating value for them based on what you know. In that way, you shift from being transaction-based to being relationship-based.

The third mind-set shift is to know that you and your team have the wisdom and experience to become a solution partner for your customer and apply that to every business interaction, every day.

I think of these shifts in mind-set as the building blocks for playing your right game of business. Now we're going to get to the UpSolutions recipe—what to do when these building blocks are in place.

CHAPTER FOUR

UPSOLUTIONS: THE RECIPE

My friend Dan wanted a shelf in his office. He went to a storage solutions store and found the shelving aisle, where he wandered around looking at all the various choices. A young clerk came up and asked him, "Can I help you?" Dan said, "No thanks."

Now, often in my experience, most clerks would walk away if someone said, "No, thank you" (if they even asked if you needed help). But instead the clerk saw Dan in the shelving aisle and asked a shelving-relevant question.

"What type of wall do you want to put a shelf up on?" At that point, Dan was in a conversation with him. "Drywall."

"Okay, what would you like to put on the shelf?" Dan told him, and the team member said, "We want to make sure the shelf is anchored properly to the drywall because of what you have on it, so I'd recommend this shelf." Dan had been looking at a $25 shelf; this one was $85. He left the store, happy with his purchase. He had gotten the right shelf for his needs and felt taken care of.

If Dan had bought the shelf he was looking at without the team member's assistance, he would have bought the $25 shelf and it would probably have fallen off the wall—maybe taking out a chunk of wall with it. Dan would have been angry and probably thought, "They sell cheap stuff!"

What happened in that conversation was simple: Dan didn't have the information to make a smart buying decision. The team member knew how to better guide him by paying attention to what it looked like he needed and asking questions.

This same interaction can happen in any business. Your customers don't know what you can do for them—they don't even know the right questions to ask. Your team has the knowledge that your customers need to make effective buying decisions. What the team needs is a recipe to be able to understand how to offer that knowledge to customers, so customers feel taken care of and make effective buying decisions. Applying the UpSolution recipe is shifting the team's mind-set from sales to understanding the market, the customers, and the unique strengths of the business.

> Applying the UpSolution recipe is shifting the team's mind-set from sales to understanding the market, the customers, and the unique strengths of the business.

Knowing how to offer UpSolutions empowers the entire team to create value by engaging customers and using the team's wisdom and experience to make a difference. This creates more team engagement and pride and generates results for the business.

Team pride is more than a nice feeling—it's a significant motivating factor for success. In his book, *Drive*, author Daniel Pink writes about the difference between workers in today's Information

Age and those of the Industrial Age. Workers in the old economy were motivated by piecemeal incentives and commissions and bonuses; add-ons based on their productivity and sales results. Today, workers' chief motivation is not financial compensation, it is a sense of *purpose*. They want to believe they matter; that they make a difference. They want to think that they are developing and improving their own skills to have more autonomy in their role so they can make a bigger impact in people's lives.[6]

This is why UpSolutions brings a team together to do its best. An UpSolution goes beyond handing a product to a customer. It is offering customers just what they need, backed by their full understanding of *why* it's the right solution for *them*.

I want to be clear about the term UpSolution—to reiterate, it is *not* what we think of as "upselling." Upselling is pushing product to increase the seller's profit. This usually means an extra or upgraded purchase beyond what the customer had already planned to buy. Upselling is, "Would you like fries with that?" It's about the seller. An UpSolution is about identifying what customers need and then fulfilling that need—it's about the buyer.

An educated buying decision based on the seller's knowledge and intention to increase value to the buyer is a win for both parties. We know what the opposite experience of being upsold is like: "I'm using a new mousse on your hair. We sell it at the register." "You can get the drill *and* the hammer for just $10 more."

Most team members don't want to feel like they're selling, and no customer wants to feel sold. UpSolutions are the absolute opposite of upselling. An UpSolution is a true *solution* for an individual customer. I like to call UpSolutions the "secret sauce" of inde-

---

6   Daniel Pink, *Drive: The Surprising Truth about What Motivates Us* (New York: Riverhead Books, 2009).

pendent business. You apply your wisdom to your customers' needs. This is exactly what the chains can't do!

The goal here, again, is to shift your employees from salespeople to customer advocates. Providing UpSolutions makes them your brand ambassadors, which in turn makes them heroes to your customers. Every team member wants to feel like a hero. UpSolutions gives everyone a chance to make someone's day.

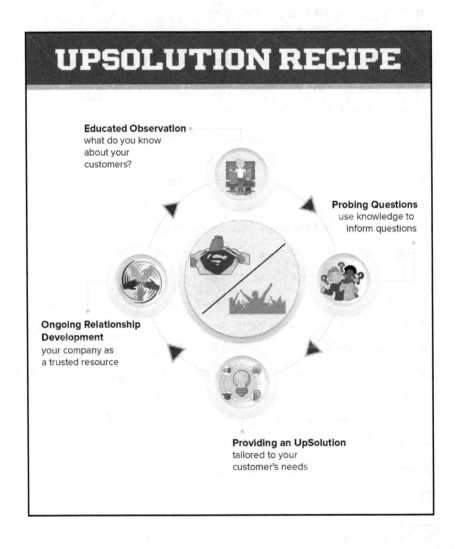

The UpSolution recipe is simple. It involves four steps:

1. *Applied wisdom through observation:* What do you know about your customer?

2. *Applied wisdom with probing questions:* Using that knowledge to inform your questions to guide customers in a buying decision

3. *Providing an UpSolution tailored to your customer's need*

4. *Ongoing relationship development:* Positioning your company as an ongoing trusted resource

APPLIED WISDOM THROUGH OBSERVATION

You begin the process when each new or returning customer comes through the door or 'entry' to your business (including landing on your website). Observing them means seeing your business through *their* eyes, *their* perspective. Based on your experience with many different customers already, when someone walks in, you already know a lot about them and what they might need. You are paying attention. It could be as simple as observing Dan in the shelving aisle: "*He's probably looking for a shelf.*" At a pharmacy counter: "*She's here to pick up a prescription.*" In a restaurant: "*They want a quiet table. Is it a special occasion?*"

What do you see as you focus on each and every customer? What do you already know about them, based on your experience with hundreds of customers? What might they need or want? Some clues:

- Did the customer gravitate to a particular area of your store?

- What does he or she appear to be looking for?

- Did the customer ask a specific question?

- What information has the customer already provided? Did he or she bring in anything to show you or call before coming in?

For instance, the team member who sold the right shelf to my friend Dan observed right away that Dan was in the shelving aisle of the store. So, he began a conversation by asking Dan shelving-relevant questions.

Remember the example in chapter 3 of a mom picking up a prescription for her feverish child? Besides a thermometer, that customer might also need electrolyte drinks, tissues, and cooling wipes. Put yourself in every customer's shoes. Ask questions. Customers may have everything they need at home already, but maybe they don't. You might identify something else that would be valuable to them. You have to dig deeper. What you already know from your experience on the job and in paying attention to each individual customer will guide you on the questions to ask.

APPLIED WISDOM WITH PROBING QUESTIONS

When asking probing questions, what you are really doing is leading customers through the decision-making process; you are helping them choose their right solution. Probing questions are specific questions that build on the knowledge you gather from that customer as you talk and listen. You are looking for detailed information about the customer's problem. This is where you dig deeper.

Say a customer comes into your electronics store looking for a cellphone. That sounds like a simple request. But consider that 201.3

million smartphones were shipped in North America in 2017.[7] Now add that smartphone sales in North America that year totaled $84 billion.[8] The array of options is clearly overwhelming. How can you help your customer choose the right one?

That depends on the questions that the team members helping the customer ask. For instance, "What's the most important thing you do on a phone? Is it email? Is it games? Calling your child after school? Uploading photos? Texting? Setting an alarm to remind you to take medication? Calling home without roaming charges when you're overseas?"

Finding out what someone is looking for and why that person needs it is the most basic information you can gather. Your questions might be determined by the customer's age. For instance, a parent might find it more important to use a cell phone to text a child; a teenager's priority might be gaming. Applied wisdom with probing questions is delving deeper for the relevant details that help you guide the customer to make an informed decision. You ask questions based on what you have observed about your customer. Remember, you are the expert!

Customers usually consider a number of factors when making an informed purchase decision. But remember that they don't always come to you knowing what they need to consider or even what to ask you about it. Asking probing questions is a critical way for your team to apply its wisdom and experience to your customers' needs.

Dan would have bought the wrong shelf without the store clerk's

---

7   "Smartphone Unit Shipments in North America from 2013 to 2017," Statista, https://www.statista.com/statistics/412212/global-smartphone-shipments-north-america.

8   "Smartphone Sales Value in North America from 2013 to 2017," Statista, https://www.statista.com/statistics/412262/global-smartphone-sales-value-north-america.

keen observation and probing questions. Knowing he bought the right shelf and *why* made him a repeat customer—and raving fan. Raving fans make for the best word-of-mouth referrals. They actively share their stories. In fact, Dan shared the story of his new shelf with me because he was so happy with the experience.

PROVIDING A CUSTOM UPSOLUTION TAILORED TO YOUR CUSTOMERS' NEEDS

When you make recommendations to customers based on the need they have communicated, you offer them a custom solution—an UpSolution—of their own choice. To help them make that choice, it is essential to communicate the value that solution provides for them—why that is the solution you recommend. Clearly communicating the value of an UpSolution naturally leads customers to appreciate your business.

Customization is key to how customers perceive the value of your business. That's why "tailor-made" is the highest compliment we give our own best choices, from cars to clothes to homes.

After taking the customer through the decision-making process, you offer your recommendation. You have educated the customer and offered choices, making recommendations through your expertise. Dan chose his shelf based on the clerk's expert recommendation. The clerk came up with his recommendation based on information from Dan: the type of wall on which the shelf would be mounted and the weight it would need to support. But before Dan could make a decision, he had to know why it was the right one. The clerk had to tell him that it suited Dan's wall and that it was strong enough to hold, in this case, Dan's books. If Dan didn't think it was the right choice, the clerk would have had to find out why, and then make a better recommendation.

It is so important that the customer understand the "why" of the recommendation—that's the difference between an option and an UpSolution.

The independent businesses that thrive today all offer customized solutions that deliver appreciated value and tell their customers exactly what they are getting.

I am a case in point. I bought my first BMW indirectly because my test drive of a Jeep was so awful. In both cases, the sales process was the deciding factor. The salesperson showing me the Jeep never asked a single question about my need for a vehicle. He kept talking about the Jeep. And like most customers, I didn't know what to ask or what I really needed. I certainly didn't know why I needed a Jeep. He didn't ask! He just wanted to deliver a sale by trying to put me through his usual sales process. It was obvious that I wasn't part of his equation when I told him I drive standard shift and he offered me an automatic to test drive. They didn't have a standard Jeep on site and he never offered to find me one. His "follow-up" was calling to see if I was ready to buy a Jeep.

Contrast that with my BMW salesperson. He had an UpSolutions approach. He asked me how I'd use the car: city or country roads? What did I need to transport? What was my budget? What safety features were important to me? Did I enjoy listening to satellite radio? What type of navigational system was I comfortable with? He asked me probing questions. I never felt pressured. I felt listened to.

Then he started designing options for me. Every time he offered me an option, he asked, "Does this fit with your needs? Are you ready to make a buying decision?" And I would say yes or no. When I said no, he asked me what didn't work about it. A day or two later, he'd follow up with more options, refined by my answers to his questions. By about the third phone call, I said, "That's it. Thank you very much. I'll be in to sign the paperwork."

I felt like he found me exactly what I wanted and I was ecstatic with it. I've now purchased three BMWs from that same dealer. An UpSolution is a process sale rather than a transactional sale. A transactional sale is, "How do I close this and get your money?" A process sale is getting your customer to "happy."

Once a team member has asked probing questions and guided the customer through the decision-making process, the UpSolution for that customer is usually obvious. That's when you make your recommendation.

When the UpSolution perfectly suits the customer, your team members become problem solvers and feel like heroes, and your customers feel completely taken care of.

The most important questions you can ask yourself before you ask for the sale is: Does my UpSolution fit my customer? Does it fit that person's need?

ONGOING RELATIONSHIP DEVELOPMENT

Earlier I talked about the sale not being the end. In fact, it's the turning point in your relationship with a customer. Happy customers want the relationship to keep going. The best thing that independent businesses can do to develop ongoing relationships is to give customers reasons to keep coming back. I can't stress the importance in the UpSolution of thinking beyond the one-time sale.

Once you've successfully taken care of a customer, ask yourself how you and your company can be a resource for that person going forward. How can you position your company as an *ongoing* solution for him or her? As customers ourselves, we have so many things to pay attention to—family, work, friends, commitments—that when we invest time and research to find a solution that works for us, we don't want to have to rethink it every time we need something. We *want* to keep coming back to our same great solution providers!

You want to give your customers the reasons they'll come back to you. That means staying in a relationship with them. Do you keep in touch with customers between their store visits? Some businesses send regular mailings, emails, or newsletters with helpful information, including sale dates. More and more businesses are using social media to stay in touch and keep customers aware of what you are offering. Whatever ongoing form of communication your business has with its customers, the purpose is to let them know how you can better take care of them. The rule of thumb to stay top-of-mind with your customers is they have to have some kind of interaction with your business at least once a month (in store, email, social media, mailing etc).

Customer retention has never been more critical to independent businesses. How you take care of your customers after their first UpSolution with you can be the difference between a customer's one-time pleasant experience or their role in your larger context: attracting and keeping *lifetime* customers.

The argument for building long-term relationships with customers is simple economics. Most industries require three transactions with the same customer to pay off your investment in acquiring their business. (your "acquisition cost.") If you only get them in one time, you're spending more money to attract them than you are generating from that sale. Plus, repeat business means raving fans who are recommending your business to others. Raving fans are a market force in themselves!

This is especially true for bricks-and-mortar businesses, particularly retail stores. Ongoing customer relationships are built on what I call retail rules, baseline practices for retail success. They go all the way back to my work experience in the bookstore. That's where I learned that certain fundamental ways of interacting with customers the first time—and every time—lead to ongoing relationships.

The first retail rule is that team members are trained to welcome everyone who enters the store. Saying hello is just the first part. Follow up! Asking, "Can I help you?" or "Are you looking for something special?" can open a conversation or cue you to a customer's preference. When customers do want something specific, take them to the section; put the item in their hand (instead of pointing, "It's over there"), and definitely don't echo the all-purpose chain store answer, "It's in Aisle Five."

It's so important to go the extra mile: if you don't have it in stock, either order it or recommend a substitute. Think "solution" instead of "sorry."

Also important is that the team give its full attention to the customers who are physically in the store. When team members talk to each other, they may not be aware that they are excluding a customer, even when that customer is right in front of them. But the customer is aware of it. We've all had the experience—as customers—of feeling overlooked or even ignored. It's rarely intentional but it's off-putting nonetheless. If the technician giving you a manicure is talking to the other technicians, you are not going to feel pampered and relaxed. This speaks to the perceived value of the service you're providing, which determines whether you make a one-time sale or build an ongoing relationship.

Another retail rule to keep customer relationships strong: thank every customer for shopping in your store. This simple act makes everyone involved feel good.

The UpSolution recipe always leaves a door open for what's next, what happens *after* a sale. For customers, there is security and satisfaction in knowing that their favorite independent business has their back. For team members, there is pride in knowing they create value in unique solutions that improve people's lives. They can make someone's day—be someone's hero—turn customers into raving fans, and unleash a powerful, collective marketing force.

The UpSolutions recipe is how you play your own right game of business. Commodity and volume-based chains cannot compete with your business because they cannot play *your* game.

CHAPTER FIVE

HEARING THE MESSAGE, NOT JUST THE WORDS

YOUR CUSTOMERS ARE ALWAYS TALKING TO YOU. ARE YOU LISTENING?

I used to shop at a popular local organic grocery store. Once, I bought a couple different flavors of chicken shish kebabs from the meat department. I was having friends over for dinner and wanted to make a special meal. Barbecued kebabs were just the thing—or so I thought. As it turned out, they had so much salt on them, they were inedible. They were so awful that even after I tried rinsing them and putting them back on the grill, they had still soaked up so much salt from the sauce that none of us could eat them. It was not my finest hour as a hostess.

The next time I was in the store, I went to the meat department to tell them about my experience. An attentive young man was working the counter. I explained that the last time I'd bought some shish kebabs, I couldn't eat them because they were too salty. And even when I'd rinsed off the marinade, they were still too salty. He said, "I'm so sorry. I'll make sure to let my manager know."

Now, that was a very *nice* response. But that was his *entire* response. What was missing was his giving me reassurance—and certainty—about the meat sold there. He could have said, "Let me take your information. My manager will follow up with you," or "Can I package something else for you so you can try it?" He was so nice—he did his job the best he knew how—but he didn't know how to get into my world. Had he gone beyond *listening* to my words to hearing my message, chances are that I'd still be buying meat from that store. As it is, I wouldn't chance it again because I have no certainty that the shish kebabs were an anomaly and not just how they prepare all their meat. I appreciated his apology, but he didn't hear what my issue was.

My issue—my message—was actually, *"My meat didn't taste good when I bought it here before and I don't feel I can buy it again if this is how you prepare it."*

Had he been trained to handle a customer complaint beyond apologizing, we would have had a different outcome. I've consistently observed that more raving fans are created when a business fixes something that's gone wrong than if everything goes right the first time. Complaints are a force field of opportunities! Turning a customer complaint around is a skill that anyone can master, and an opportunity for your team and business to shine as you show the value you create and offer.

Sean Lenehan owns Lenehan Wealth Management Group in Windsor Ontario. He has turned customer complaints and challenges into growth opportunities. Their philosophy is to "embrace the chaos." When something goes wrong or a client is upset, it sets the stage for their team to shine and demonstrate their value.

> ## LENEHAN WEALTH MANAGEMENT GROUP
> ### Policies on Handling Client Requests and Upsets
>
> When a client:
>
> 1. proactively reaches out to you. This is a priority over all other "to dos." Why? If clients take the time out of their busy day to reach out to you, then it's obviously a priority for them! This is an opportunity to shine and demonstrate the value you bring regarding "service."
>
> 2. client reaches out proactively yet, in addition, they are "out of balance." This situation is the utmost opportunity to demonstrate our "unique offering." If the clients are angry, agitated, anxious—whatever the "negative" emotion(s) are that they are displaying—this is an opportunity to put yourself at the top of the value chain. Almost everyone in this world places value on those who can assist to bring one "back to balance."
>
> How?
>
> 1. Listen … don't tell
>
> 2. Your first words should be acknowledgement of their feelings, even if you feel they may be wrong—that's irrelevant at the moment. 3) Verbalize "empathy" for how they are feeling, not for the situation. You are not accepting blame but simply allowing the client to feel heard and acknowledged—this is 90 percent of the battle completed!

3. Repeat what the client has stated as his/her "concern, issue, and reasons" for being upset. Feel free to ask questions that engage the "rational mind," rather then the "emotional mind" where they most likely are currently situated. Ask the client "what is it in your mind that would make this situation resolved?" Is it a rational achievable solution or not? Remind the client that you will do all that is within your control and try to influence the situation as best as you can, yet also remind them of any issues at hand that you cannot control or influence. This allows for you to get expectations back to a rational place.

4. Ask if it would be okay by them that you take these issues and review with your team. Upon review and analysis from all parties needed, you will get back to the client. (Note: Give the client a date you will get back to them with update or a solution; this also takes away anxiety.)

5. Once you follow up with recommended solutions, be sure to ask the client if he/she is happy with how you handled the situation.

Remember, there is no better gift than making someone feel better. The ability to assist someone out of a "negative" emotional state and back to "balance" is rare and an extremely valuable talent!

This is where we shift gears. In the first sections of this book, we've focused on the relationship-based customer mind-set and the UpSolutions recipe. In this part, we get into the skills you need to make it all work.

Your customers are actively communicating with you every day. Are you listening? They are your best source of market research! They tell you who they are, what's important to them, what goes into their buying decisions, what they are most looking for, and more. If you just listen, really listen, to what your customers are saying to you, all that marketing intelligence is available every day in your business.

Yet many companies miss this opportunity. They miss it because the team is engaging with the customers' words but not absorbing the message behind them. My experience has shown me that rarely has a team been trained to listen for the message being communicated. We know how to respond to statements like, "Thanks for getting me that so fast." ("You're welcome.") "How long will it take to get my dry cleaning back?" ("Tuesday, 1 p.m.") "Do you have this in my size?" ("Let me look for you.")

Hearing and clearly understanding the messages that comprise your best market research is the first essential skill you need to position your business as a solution partner for your customer. Chances are, depending on the size of your business, it's your team members who have the most contact with customers. When the owner feels disconnected from customers, and vice versa, it's often because a team member has not been trained to hear and capture the message—and then communicate it to management.

> Everything a customer says to a team member or the owner communicates something that is important to that customer.

Everything a customer says to a team member or the owner communicates something that is important to that customer. When patients thank a pharmacy for filling their prescription quickly, they're communicating that their time is very important to them. When customers want an ETA on their dry cleaning, they want to know if they'll be able to wear it to an event. When they ask, "Do you have this in my size?" they're often saying, "Will this look good on me?"

The most common question asked at Disney's Magic Kingdom is "What time is the 2pm parade?". Sounds silly! But if you are paying attention to what the customers are really asking (and Disney's 'cast' has been well trained for) what parents are really asking is when to be there to get their children a front-row view.

"Yes" or "No" answers stop the conversation. You hear the message when you listen below the surface. Then, your responses become, "We're here for you"; "I remember, you have a special event coming up;" and "I think you'll look great in this dress" (or, "Here's something you'll look even better in"). Paying attention to your customers' messages is critical to positioning as their solution partner. And that means the whole team, not just the owner, as it's often the team members who have daily interactions with customers. Capturing that message is the most critical part of every customer encounter. Teaching your team to listen for it is, in my opinion, the most critical part of their training. Besides putting everybody in your business on the same page, listening for the message lets you discuss your business as a cohesive, confident, and *invested* team.

When customers ask a price question, especially at the beginning of an interaction, they are usually communicating they don't have the information to make an effective decision. Learn to celebrate when customers ask you about cost or price—this is your opportunity to showcase why to choose you! "Before I answer that let me ask you a few questions to make sure I'm giving you the information you need."

We all know how frustrated we get when we think other people aren't listening to or hearing what we are saying. The problem is that we usually forget that frustration when we are the ones listening! If you look at your business through your customers' eyes and enter their world—if you listen to the message they are sharing and not just their words—they'll tell you exactly what they want and what they need. That will give you a natural marketplace advantage. You can hear things that your competitors can't because they are focused on transactions.

Customer data comes back to you in so many ways. It's communicated by compliments and thank-you notes, suggestions/ideas for improvement, and frequently asked questions (which are really requests). The most uncomfortable and often the most important are complaints, upsets, and mistakes, which give your team opportunities to be heroes by fixing them. The goal in training is twofold: to ensure your team is actively listening all the time, and to gather and communicate the strategic information they're hearing about what pleases and displeases customers—information you can use to improve your business.

First, let's break down each of those communication channels to get beyond the words to the messages. Then, I'll show you how to use all the information you've collected to make your company the clear, leading-edge standout in your field.

HOW YOU GET THE MESSAGE

COMPLIMENTS AND THANK-YOU NOTES

It's wonderful when you get immediate and direct positive feedback from customers while they are still in the store. This feedback can come at any point in the customer's experience. For example, a customer entering the store may compliment the environment and the music. You get the message immediately that your customer is having a pleasant experience and that these details are what that person wants and are important enough to for him or her to notice and share that positive reaction with you.

A compliment invites a warm response: people say, "Well, isn't that nice of them to write a thank-you note!" But they often miss the real weight of the compliment; those notes aren't just about being *nice*, they're giving you valuable information on what, exactly, pleases the sender. When that information comes from your target audience customers, you want to pay attention and even highlight that more in your business.

The reason that many businesses display the thank-you cards and notes they receive from customers: pride! Everyone can see the business's pride and connection to its customers. I have even seen email printouts taped up on a wall! Could there be a better message behind the words? Gratitude uplifts everyone—the owner, the team, even other customers who see them. One veterinarian I know has cards and notes pinned with a photo of the sender's animal on bulletin boards in every exam room of the practice. That show of gratitude is reassuring for customers that their own family pet is in the right hands. Plus, looking at cute animals can be calming in an anxious situation. (Well, maybe for the people, not so much the pet!) One pharmacy in Iowa uses the store's big interior pillars to showcase customer compliments and thank-yous. The pillars are covered with notes, Post-its, and cards of gratitude—even happy family photos.

SUGGESTIONS/IDEAS FOR IMPROVEMENT

When customers have suggestions and ideas for improving your business, it's because they want to refine something about their experience, and they value you enough to make the request. For example, if you're a retailer with high shelves and some of your target customers are short (a constant frustration in toy stores, to the relief of customers' parents), they might suggest that you place items more conveniently within their reach or make them more accessible. Your target customers' suggestions provide you with openings to give them even more helpful service and your business greater visibility. So, make it *easy* for your customers to share their suggestions and ideas for improvement, both in-store and online. Pay special attention to the ones that come in from your target audiences, the two to five groups of "right fit" customers you serve. Be especially aware of the *message* behind the words. People who take the time to make positive suggestions to your business want to remain—or become—raving fans and returning customers. Also pay attention to what they *don't* like in doing business with you. Customers only tell you what they care about, both positive and negative.

What happens when you can't implement a frequent suggestion or don't see its value to your business? Take the case of a small, neighborhood women's boutique with a strict return policy: store credit only, within ten days, with a receipt. The owner, in business for thirty years, has often heard customers ask that she relax the return policy. This would seem like a clear case of becoming a solution partner to customers, but in this case, the owner turns over inventory very quickly. That's part of what makes her store so unique. Even ten days later, a returned item may be gone from the racks, and she doesn't want the hassle of handling returns. For her, the return policy simplifies the paperwork for a very small team, makes her business run more efficiently, and doesn't cost her a significant enough loss in sales to change it.

This example raises the question, "How do you communicate 'No' to your customers?" My tried-and-true tip for smoothing over their disappointment and annoyance is that when delivering bad news or not providing what a customer has asked for, you offer them choices.

If, as was the case with the boutique owner, you don't implement a suggestion, then you have to come up with a creative way to position the "why not"—and make sure every team member knows how to state it. The boutique team might, for instance, say something like, "Our commitment is to have new and interesting items in stock for our customers so that what you're wearing is always unique. We depend on fast turnover to keep things new and different for you." Always give them a "why" that speaks to *them*. Offering a *choice* puts the customer back in control of the shopping experience. And, you can offer exceptions to some policies. The boutique team is empowered to extend the return policy for a few days if the item is a gift, or extend store credit for a portion of the purchase price if the customer doesn't have a receipt.

Flexibility shows that you have gotten the message behind the words. "I suggest you change your strict return policy" is actually, "I want you to make it easy for me to buy stuff from you." When you answer customer gripes by communicating what's in it for *them*, your customers will be more receptive to hearing, "I'm very sorry, but no."

FREQUENTLY ASKED QUESTIONS

Your answers to questions frequently asked by customers are a key part of your marketing communications. While team members should answer every question that a customer asks, when a pattern emerges, it's time to make your answers a visible part of your message.

The best way to integrate frequently asked questions (FAQs) into your business marketing is to answer them publicly, both on your website and social media. Ideally, your website copy should answer every question that a customer might ask about your business. There should also be a way for visitors to the site to ask questions that are not integrated into your web content or accessed by your FAQ page. Team training should include regular updates on requested information so that members are prepared to answer any question (both online and in-store) that would help customers make a buying decision.

I first saw the power of using FAQs as a communications strategy years ago when a friend of mine built a fundraising website. He'd been nominated for "Man of the Year" in his area and had a fundraising target he wanted to reach for the event's cause. So, he built a website specifically to raise funds and invited questions about his effort. Every question submitted had an answer on the website within twenty-four hours. He posted the actual question and its answer or he integrated its message into the site content. That way, visitors had questions answered before they were even asked. He exceeded his fundraising target, proving along the way that every question tells you what someone needs to know to make a buying decision.

When you have insight into that message—what will prompt your customers to do business with you—you have struck marketing gold. The words customers use to ask their questions, to unlock their wants or needs—what pleases them, what frustrates them, what inspires them—can be your marketing language. For example, a restoration company that repairs the damage to homes after a flood or fire "putting your life and home back together one piece at a time." Or a pharmacy's byline: "When you absolutely positively want to feel better." Or a horse farrier: "putting the proper motion back in your horse from the ground up."

The best websites pay attention to every question that's submitted.

And, their answers always give visitors a "why" that positions everything the business does as an advantage to them.

CASE STUDY: ALLBIRDS

Allbirds (allbirds.com) was started by Tim Brown and Joey Zwillinger with the idea of using natural materials to create the world's most comfortable shoe ("Comfort that comes naturally"). They had an innovative product idea and needed to determine how to break into a crowded (and commodity-based) marketplace. They chose a direct-to-consumer approach with a fun, accessible, and funky website, great customer service, and a product that people love. What I found fascinating is the attention to detail—every part of the purchase and delivery of the product enhances the unique value of the shoes and has the customer feel they are part of a movement of comfortable, environmentally friendly footwear. The packaging is simple with quirky bird graphics and messaging that has me feel as if I'm connecting with a live person. I loved my Allbirds so much I bought a pair as a gift. I picked a good color but the wrong size—no problem. They have an easy and free exchange process—the exchange created an even better appreciation of their customer service and makes online ordering risk free. They have done a brilliant job of paying attention to their customers and incorporating marketing language to have you feel as if they are talking directly to you.

Often retail stores fear online competition. Allbirds is a great example of a retail business using online resources to build their brand awareness and create a distribution model that has been so successful they have now opened stores in major cities.

Again, it's key to understand what motivated the question—the message behind it. What is the question telling you? What's important to the customer?

Take a question as simple as, "How much do you charge?" When people ask that, they're telling you that they don't know the information they need to make an effective buying decision. If they don't know that, then their decision will be based on price. But that's not your right game of business! If your customers don't know why to choose you, they choose the lowest perceived price. So, your job is to clearly communicate why they should choose your business.

The most common first question from a new prospective customer calling in to a carpet cleaning business I've worked with is "What do you charge?". The team has been trained to respond with "Let me ask you a couple of questions so I can answer that for you". Then they lead into probing questions to find out what the person really needs—why they want their carpets cleaned. It's never about the carpets—it's about maintaining home value, healthy living, pets and children and stains, company coming over, about to sell their home.

Your answers to every question from a customer or prospect must convey that *you* understand what *they* need to know to be able to make an effective buying decision. When a prospective customer asks you how much you charge, then your team must be trained and ready to reply, "Before I answer that, let me ask you a couple of questions. I need more information to be able to give you an accurate price."

Now you've positioned yourself as a business that asks questions that differentiate customer needs. These are the probing questions that allow you to guide customers to make effective buying decisions.

WISHES AND REQUESTS

When target customers ask you for something special, do you go the extra mile? There are so many small ways to do this that seem huge to the person asking: being mindful that the customer is in a hurry; wrapping the gift; helping those with physical challenges move around the store; slicing the bread very thin; giving directions; and, in at least one case I know of, keeping the dog company outside while he was tied to a bench as his owner shopped.

Every wish and request from a customer is an opportunity to redouble your value to them. This is when you have a bonus chance to get *your* message across—that you go the distance and then some for your customers. If a customer can't get there to pick something up before you close, that's when you offer to hold the item, deliver it, or take the payment information over the phone. These acts may not be standard procedure for your business, but they convey the message that you not only value customers' business, you care about *them*.

You won't be able to accommodate every wish and special request, of course, but there are other ways to transform a customer's need or want into positive experiences with your business. Coupons, special orders, calling them when an item comes in: all of these send the message that you and your team are their solution partners.

COMPLAINTS, UPSETS, AND MISTAKES

This is my favorite subject when it comes to hearing the message behind the words. Complaints are one of your most valuable communication resources. A complaint is a door opening to the opportunity to create a raving fan. Most people slam the door shut by making the customer wrong. But when your entire team is trained to handle complaints well, every one of them is a chance to shine. Even the dreaded Yelp one-star review. When you create an environment in which your customers feel confident telling you what they like and don't like, they give you the chance to make things right. Seize it.

First, here is what *not* to do when a customer has a complaint: for years, a friend of mine who has horses had been getting the same herbal tincture for them from the same store. Then the business hired a new herbalist. Suddenly her orders were wrong. She'd been explicit about what she needed multiple times. At $160 a bottle, this wasn't a small purchase for her; in fact, she'd confirmed it three times on the phone. The wrong product was sent anyway. When she called to say she received the wrong product, the herbalist said she ordered the wrong product—it was the customer's fault. When the corrected tincture was sent, it was cloudy and her vet advised against using it. Now the business had an annoyed customer who no longer trusted what they offered.

It was the shop's perfect opportunity to turn her into a raving fan; instead, the store lost a customer. She posted a negative review online and stopped going there.

If you've ever wondered whether online reviews actually mean anything to a business, consider this: nearly 70 percent of prospective customers read online reviews of a business before making a purchase there.[9] And it's not just Yelp; it's Yahoo, Angie's List, Facebook, and many other sites.

One good thing about negative reviews—the occasional one, I

---

9   Melinda Emerson, "How to Turn Around a Bad Review Online Successfully," Small Business Trends, April 14, 2015, https://smallbiztrends.com/2014/06/how-to-turn-around-a-bad-review-online.html.

mean, not regular issues: they make your profile look "more real"[10] and give you the opportunity to reply and resolve the customer's issue, the happy results of which they can also share online. When planning a trip I regularly read reviews for AirBnB places to stay. I'm interested in seeing the overall reviews and if there is a negative one, how it was responded to.

All bad social media reviews are perfect opportunities to "lean in" when a customer complains. If this happens to you, you would turn it around the same way you would handle an in-store complaint: apologize and work to solve your customer's problem. A negative review that leads you to fix something and earn the customer's gratitude *and* loyalty ultimately has more impact than a first-time positive review.

When the owner or a team member responds to a bad review with, "I am so sorry that happened to you. Let me dig into this and follow up with you. I'd like to correct this," and then follows through, you become a hero. If you don't take the opportunity to answer at all, either in person, by phone, or online, then your attitude to customers and prospects will be seen as indifference.

There is a really great book called *A Complaint Is a Gift: Recovering Customer Loyalty When Things Go Wrong*, by Janelle Barlow and Claus Moller, now in its second edition. The authors break down responding to a complaint into a step-by-step formula. The first thing to know is that complaints are one of the most important forms of customer communication—and almost no business handles them well. Why? Because a complaint usually comes with an emotional force. It takes energy to both give and receive a complaint, and it's

---

10   Ibid.

not comfortable for either party.[11]

We're not used to thinking about a complaint as constructive communications, but it really *is* a gift when somebody takes the time to make one. When you disregard it—or miss the opportunity it holds—you lose valuable information for your business success. Discomfort with complaints prevents growth and limits perceived value. It also discounts the complaining customer at the expense of missing the message.[12]

As Barlow and Moller point out, a step as simple as thanking someone for a complaint changes the dynamic of the interaction. How? You immediately accomplish two things: putting that person at ease and giving yourself a chance to catch your breath. The customer feels heard and you feel more open and receptive. "Thank you" is the pivotal tool for using complaints to strengthen your business. Be sure to add *why* you're thanking them so your response has substance. For instance, "Thank you for letting me know. I can't do anything about it if I don't hear about it." Then, find out what else you need to know to correct it, if you can. If you can't do that on the spot, let the person know what you intend to do and when you'll get back to them. Then, do it and check that they're satisfied with the result. Strive for consistency in handling complaints; you and your team can identify common mistakes and develop responses for these that the entire team can be trained to execute.

When you respond to complaints by listening for the message, the customer feels heard and taken care of. And this is the experience they're *not* getting in chains and national stores. Indifference accounts for loss of customers.

---

11 Janelle Barlow and Claus Moller, *A Complaint Is a Gift: Recovering Customer Loyalty When Things Go Wrong,* 2nd ed. (San Francisco: Berrett-Koehler Publishers, 2008).

12 Ibid.

Everyone, it seems, has an airline story, or several, they could tell to illustrate this point. On my most recent trip, flying to Los Angeles from Toronto on our way to New Zealand, a distance of more than 2,100 miles, there were two washrooms for everyone sitting in Economy. One of them was out of commission because it had no toilet paper. My friend Lisa went to tell the flight attendants, who were all at the back of the plane, chatting. They seemed annoyed at the interruption. One said, "We can't do anything about that."

Apparently, the plane was stocked on the ground and they don't carry extra supplies. So, for the entire trip, everyone lined up for the one washroom that had paper. Lisa said, "They just *didn't care*."

Indifference isn't just a buzz killer, it's a business killer. I heard one story about a shopper who won't go back to a major department store because she couldn't get a single team member to care that a mouse was nosing around the floor in women's wear. She later told a friend, "They all acted like what's *my* problem that I can't deal with a rodent?" She never went back.

Every single example we just went through of unresolved customer complaints was a missed opportunity for growth and positioning value by appreciating the customer, hearing what they were saying and then creating and communicating a solution.

HOW YOU USE THE MESSAGE

When you collect and capture customer feedback on an ongoing basis, the next step is to unlock the information and discuss customer-based strategies built upon what you've gathered. You'll want to review the content, separate the message from the words, share it with your team at regularly scheduled staff meetings, and use your analysis as the basis for future decisions.

The reason team buy-in is so important is that in most businesses, it's the team members who have daily contact with customers. So, if they aren't trained to listen to customers, they're missing both the words *and* the message. If the team doesn't capture and communicate the message, the line of communication is broken. That works both ways: the owner *and* team must process feedback and turn it into action. And, it applies to both positive and negative data.

Here's an example of how customer feedback became a call to action at one company. At my friends' custom carpet and restoration business, customers consistently told workers what a great job they did cleaning carpets. Still, when it came time to filling out a post job review or testimonial for the business, very few customers did. When asked why, the answer was usually, "I don't have time." Delving deeper, the owners learned the message behind the words: *"The job is done and talking about it is not important to me."*

But the business wanted referrals; they were important for the company's growth. How could they get them when their satisfied customers said, "Thanks for your service, but I've moved on"? How could the business make referrals seem important to their current customers?

It couldn't. But the team members could explain their position upfront when the job started. Their idea for improving the rate of referral was to strategically communicate with the customer before the work was done. The dialogue went something like this: "If you're happy with the work we do, please know that our business, like all businesses, grows based on referrals. So, if you can think of someone to tell about your experience with us, we'll throw in a gift card."

Any time you analyze the messages in a customer's feedback, you can come up with an improvement idea. Find a way to make it happen. The company soon found another gem in customer messaging. After a number of customers declined add-on services—"I don't need Scotchgard," "I don't need [blank] service done"—the team discovered that was because either the customers had had a poor previous experience, or they didn't know the value of what was being offered to them. The service provider knew, though—if you've got young children and/or pets in the house, you need Scotchgard! Look for the ways you too can educate your customers based on their messages.

But how do you act on conflicting feedback, as is often the case? The first thing to look at is: *Are they my target audience clients?* Disney World is a great example of how to identify target audiences. They reach out to young families (children's entertainment), young adults (group activities where people mingle), and seniors (nostalgia-inspired experiences). You can see in their advertising that they know the lifetime value of a client.

Even though those are three very different target audiences, something links them all: they seek out life experiences that promise fun and wonder (even when the wonder is nostalgic). Disney is built on providing that experience. It's not an amusement park—it's Walt Disney World.

The last piece in message analysis and follow-up is always: *What did I learn from that? How can the team grow and learn from that?*

Here are my tips to develop your skills in hearing the message, not just the words:

If you're giving a customer news they don't want to hear, offer a choice. For instance, a common issue at pharmacies is that the prescription isn't ready yet. This is not what patients want to hear. It could have nothing to do with the speed of the pharmacist—it could be something going on with the insurance company. Patients don't care why; they just know that their prescription is not ready as promised. The business can offer to deliver it, call the patient when it is ready, give them a one-day supply so no meds are missed, etc. Always provide a choice when you can't provide immediate customer satisfaction.

It might not be your fault, but it is your problem. This is a Disney slogan that I think every company should adopt. There are lots of things that happen in a business that are not the team's fault, but because they're interacting with customers, it *is* their problem. Train every employee to be a solution partner. When you hear the message, find a way to solve the issue for the customer—and communicate, communicate, communicate.

Identify the common mistakes in your business and practice dealing with them. Have regular team meetings to discuss what is being communicated in customer feedback and use the messages to fuel continuous improvement, solidify customer relationships, and look for growth opportunities.

Make your customers feel good, not bad. When addressing a customer's issue with your business, making the customer think he or she did something wrong, crazy, or stupid, or that they're lying, is bad for business. At that point, the issue becomes how you *handle* the issue. That includes online communication. Thank customers who post positive reviews. Respond to negative reviews by investigating the complaint, making the customer whole, and engaging with the critic to make sure you've resolved the issue.

A complaint is a gift. You're being judged not only on the quality of your products or services but also on your connection to customers. Everything you do either contributes to or detracts from your relationship with them.

To keep your business positioned on the leading edge in your marketplace, you need top skills in customer communication. Your customer is always talking to you—are you listening to the message, not just the words? Is your team? Train team members to hear and capture customer communication, especially with complaints. It's a good idea to discuss customer communication as part of your entire team communications structure at regularly scheduled meetings.

Once you've mined and used the data from customer messages, you're in a terrific position to keep the customer interaction and relationship going. How? There are many ways to nurture it, among them newsletters, email announcements (great for sale days), customer loyalty programs, social media etc. I'll discuss these in depth in the next chapter.

Now that you've mastered the skill of translating words into messages and messages into solutions, your business has a well-developed natural market advantage. Next, let's look at the customer's real-time experience of your business.

CHAPTER SIX

TOTAL CUSTOMER FOCUS AND EXPERIENCE

Hearing the message behind the words is only one skill that team members need to cultivate raving fans. *Really* understanding what customers communicate calls for training and supporting teams to be consciously aware of that and use it to deliver consistent experiences to customers. It is also critical for everyone on the team to understand *how* customers *already* experience the business to bridge the distance between the value we *think* we provide and how customers perceive us. In this chapter, we take customer awareness to the next level, building a bridge from verbal communication to connect us directly to the customer's world. In fact, we need to *immerse* ourselves in the customer's world. Welcome to Total Customer Focus and Experience.

We use two wonderful models to do this: the front-stage/back-stage model that comes from theater; and the on-brand/off-brand model that marketers use to refine branded customer service. These are both simple strategies for owners to train and reinforce among team members. They make it easy for the team to always—and eventually automatically—see things from the customer's perspective. They are the tools you need to succeed at it.

Additionally, we use a "touchpoint scorecard" to help you identify what a customer would feel as they experience your business. This is such an important viewpoint that I created the tool to make it easier for both owners and team members to measure the different ways that customers interact with your business. You'll see how it works later in the chapter.

We're all comfortable thinking from our own perspective; what we know, what we're used to, maybe even how the people we know think. But thinking from our own perspective keeps us in our own heads. Getting inside someone's else's head—understanding *their* perspective—comes more naturally to some people than others, but we all have the ability to develop this skill. It takes practice to put yourself in someone else's mind-set and be aware of what's important to *them*. It is critical to an independent company's success.

HELLO, I AM ...

I'm a big advocate of using name tags in business. Perhaps the most important reason is that knowing someone's name instantly makes customers feel connected to another real person, a professional who is there to help them. Sometimes the name tag is all it takes to begin a relationship with a team member; just saying your name doesn't mean the customer will remember it! Also, you want team members to be highly visible. We all know the sense of frustration we get as customers when you feel like there's no one around to help you. Team members are front stage; name tags may be the introduction to "on-brand." In businesses where several team members interact with customers—for instance, hair salons—customers may hear several names, and when they don't remember them, they feel uncomfortable. Not knowing someone's name creates a barrier. My friends Len and Annette give all team members in their carpet restoration business photo IDs—very important when you go into customers' homes, as their team does. Uniforms may or may not feel right for a business, but with name tags, you can never go wrong.

FRONT STAGE/BACK STAGE

The first business model to share with your team to best align your business's value consistently to the customer experience is called Front Stage/Back Stage. Think of a theater: there's what you see and experience on stage while seated in the audience: Lights! Singing! Dancing! Then there's everything you don't see: the ropes and pulleys, the sets and props, the makeup room, the bookkeeper's office. Front stage in a business is everything about that business that touches your customer's experience. Back stage is everything that happens 'behind the scenes' for the business to function and create the front stage experience. What your customers aren't—and shouldn't be—aware of. It's an easy concept to train your team on, easy to remember, and easy to reinforce.

Front stage/back stage comes from the book, *The Experience Economy: Work Is Theater & Every Business a Stage,* by B. Joseph

Pine and James H. Gilmore.[13] In it, the authors discuss the concept of "front stage/back stage"—again, the part of your business that customers see versus the part that's hidden from them.

While the idea isn't new—*The Experience Economy* was first published in 1999—it has enduring value for businesses that want to escape feeling commoditized.

The authors found that people are willing to pay more money for an experience from businesses that don't compete on price if its perceived value is greater to them than the cost savings. Going strictly by price means commoditization.

Viewing your business this way has a profound impact on how you set up the front stage and separate the back stage from customers' experience. Strategic Coach, the leading business coaching program for entrepreneurs, turned this idea into a model that is part of their coaching program.[14]

So, what is a front-stage experience in business and how does it figure into aligning your business to the value you create for customers?

From your own life's experience, you know from plays or concerts that the audience is focused on what's happening right in front of them. You experience magic on that stage. And you're blissfully unaware that people are changing costumes, scanning their lines again, and trading signals to move sets into place. There's a massive amount of equipment and activity that happens back stage and, barring unintended mishaps, you won't see it. To see it breaks the spell of the immersive theater experience.

---

13 B. Joseph Pine and James H. Gilmore, *The Experience Economy: Work Is Theater & Every Business a Stage* (Cambridge, Massachusetts: Harvard Business School Press, 1999).

14 The Front Stage/Back Stage Model® Strategic Coach®, https://www.strategic-coach.com/.

For instance, in the musical *The Lion King*, when gazelles bound down the aisle, you completely forget that you're not seeing real animals but people in costumes. Another play, *War Horse*, uses huge puppets to tell the story. There are two actors maneuvering inside each "horse." They do such a phenomenal job that the audience feels an emotional connection to these puppet horses.

But what would happen if halfway through a show the curtain fell down? Seeing the back stage would completely disrupt the magic that had been created on the front stage! And even if the actors or crew did a phenomenal job of recovering from the surprise, the magic would most likely be gone from that performance.

In business, the front stage is everything that happens that your customers experience, both inside and outside your store, with your team members, packaging, and even the visual experience of your website. How your team members answer the phone, whether they look and act professional, how quickly the checkout line moves: all this is the front stage for your customers.

The back stage is scheduling, punching time cards, taking inventory, stocking the shelves, etc. Every business has both a front stage and a back stage. When something jarring occurs to disrupt a customer's positive experience of your business—say two employees begin arguing about whose turn it is to take a break—it's as though the curtain suddenly dropped for your customers and you must work to reengage them.

The back stage can easily take front stage if team members lose their awareness of customers. For instance, the front stage in a pharmacy is everything a customer can see, starting from the street as they approach the store and then when they walk inside. The pharmacy counter is the main show; customers see the pharmacist behind it working to fill their prescriptions.

The problem with a counter, anywhere, is that it can become a collecting place. It's easy to put one thing down on it—and all of a sudden, stuff multiplies: mail, files, boxes. Sorting back-stage items has suddenly become front stage because the customer sees clutter and chaos. We tend to overlook what's right in front of us when we're not paying attention, but the customer sees everything. What are they seeing? Shipments coming in and parked "for now" in your store's front stage. Products that need to be moved or reshelved. Boxes stacked up. Clothing, unfolded and scattered, waiting to be put out.

The back stage can show itself in other ways too: when you get to the cashier and he's too busy talking with a colleague to notice you. Or you call a company and get sent to voicemail jail. Then call back, get transferred from person to person, and then hung up on.

I'll never forget seeing one colossal back-stage intrusion into the front stage. Once, on a road trip, at a highway rest stop, I went to McDonald's. While I was waiting in line to place my order, one of the team members came up to the manager, who was working the counter, to get his okay for her own lunch. The manager started to berate her about how much she was eating, even checking the level of Coke in her cup! Belittling a team member in front of customers who were about to order! I felt so bad for the team member.

The front stage requires your *constant awareness* because it has a direct impact on the quality of your customer's experience. Is your front stage all it can be? Does everything connected with your business that your customer sees firsthand contribute to a positive experience?

The classic example of front-stage awareness is Disney World. Now, I'm not suggesting that every business strive to be Disney-fied with a front stage like the Magic Kingdom. But Disney perfectly illustrates how guests become so immersed in a positive experience, where everything is aligned to support that, that they will happily pay between $103-$129 per person to spend a day there. And it is always full. Because it's not an amusement park, it's Disney World! Specifically, it's Disney's front stage.

An example of front-stage awareness in restaurants is dining at a "kitchen table," where diners pay a premium to see the "show:" chefs making the meal. What had been a back-stage experience, cooking the meal to order, now becomes a front-stage experience as the kitchen moves into the dining room and diners watch the action. The hectic activity of a restaurant kitchen is still there, only it's orchestrated to engage customers.

Normally, you would never see this, unless you watch television shows like *Top Chef*. There, from the ruckus of a restaurant's back-stage kitchen, emerges a splendid plate of food, which is then served front stage in the dining room.

But chef Charlie Trotter, who once owned an upscale restaurant in Chicago, turned the restaurant model on its head in the mid-1990s. He created the experience of his restaurant *around the food*. He created the kitchen table concept, which turned the normal back stage of the kitchen into a front stage, where his kitchen team was putting on a show, preparing food for everyone in the dining room, in full view. (To make this happen, they had to do all the prep work in advance, before the doors opened.) By turning dining into theater, he consciously created an aligned experience for customers. It was so popular that the restaurant, and especially the kitchen table, sold out so quickly that you had to make reservations months in advance. It became the rage for the industry.

Not every restaurateur who tried to implement the concept of the kitchen table was as successful. I went to a restaurant in Toronto that advertised a kitchen table. There was a table in the kitchen, but that didn't make it a front-stage experience; the staff couldn't understand how to create *theater*. The owner yelled and swore at the kitchen team; the staff dropped things on the floor; the sound of dishes clattering interrupted conversation. This back stage was chaos—and we all got to experience it. So, the restaurant had a front stage—the kitchen—but wasn't operating it with the awareness of creating an *aligned* experience for customers. It was an example of unawareness of how diners experienced the restaurant. And, the owner clearly wasn't aware of how to make the kitchen table work.

Are you consciously aware of the front stage and back stage in your business? If you and your team are not creating a consistent front-stage experience that's aligned with the value of your business, then you will be commoditized, forced to compete on price.

Independent businesses have the strategic advantage of being able to design a front-stage experience that aligns with their value. This alignment is the ingredient that leads to repeat business and raving fans. It's the difference between a price-based versus experience-based economy.

Hand-in-glove with the front-stage/back-stage model for total customer focus is a concept first presented in the book, *Branded Customer Service: The New Competitive Edge* by Janelle Barlow (author of *A Complaint is a Gift*) and Paul Stewart. The authors describe the process of training your team to be "on-brand" rather than "off-brand."[15] An on-brand experience is any experience you create that reinforces your business's value to its customers. An off-brand experience is any experience you create that takes value away from your business. Let's take a closer look at that.

---

15 Janelle Barlow and Paul Stewart, *Branded Customer Service: The New Competitive Edge* (New York: Berrett-Koehler Publishers, 2006).

ON- AND OFF-BRAND EXPERIENCES

Loyal customers and raving fans are products of three integrated factors: they must like the product or service you sell; they must like the atmosphere of your business; and they must like the real-time experience they have when doing business with you. When you hit all three, your customers trust you, feel connected to you, and develop a relationship with you.

Your awareness of the front stage goes beyond keeping your space clean and ordered; it's about providing "on-brand" customer experiences that constantly reinforce the value your company is providing. These are the experiences that engage customers with your brand and create a bond between you and them. Everything about their experience doing business with you should advance their sense of connectedness. If something about it is out of place—say, clutter on the pharmacy counter—that suggests "chaotic" to customers, which takes away from the front-stage, on-brand message you really want to send, which is, "We're here to help you with your healing and sense of well-being."

Here, I'm reminded of my college job at the bookstore: The manager showed the team how to create an on-brand experience by training us to follow specific practices. For instance, we were to greet everyone who entered the store, and then ask if we could help them and if they were looking for a specific book. If we had it, we'd take them to the section and put the book in their hand, not point to "over there." If we didn't have the book, we'd order it for them or make an alternate suggestion. If there was even one customer in the store, team members had to refrain from having side conversations that customers could hear. These simple ways to serve customers are what created our on-brand customer experience.

Even the sign on the back of the stockroom door that reminded us to leave our personal issues back there when we went out to serve customers taught us the difference between front stage and back stage. I am sure that these models led not only to the store's sales success but also to how well we worked as a team, and how much fun we had doing it.

In a front-stage, on-brand experience, everything is aligned with the value your business creates in taking care of customers. Even the dirtiest car repair garage can have a clean waiting area with coffee for customers and have your car ready on time. This is all part of building trust and relationships. Connectedness makes us feel known and appreciated. At the same time, it all reinforces the value you provide to customers, which is your game of business. You want them to have a fantastic experience with you—with each experience building their trust, sense of connection, and relationship with you. Feeling valued and cared for are the ingredients that lead to repeat business and raving fans. This is a front-stage, on-brand experience.

Anything about the customer experience that is out of alignment—anything that is negative or jarring to them—is an off-brand experience. These experiences detract from your value and take away your business advantage.

Some triggers for an experience that feels off-brand to a customer are obvious: rude employees, a too-long wait in line or on hold, and issues with damaged merchandise. But there can also be subconscious triggers, say, seeing cobwebs in a doorway. (Dirt anywhere communicates "unhealthy." It sends people right back out the door.)

Every touchpoint of client contact communicates an on-brand or an off-brand message, based on whether it supports or detracts from what you want to convey. For example, faded posters in a store window tell passersby that their time has already come and gone. If they are out of synch with what's current (say, a Christmas poster still up in March), people stop looking at the window. Always bring awareness to what's displayed in your prime real estate, including window space, the ends of shelving units, and endcaps in the store. They need to be changed at least monthly or you will be advertising a dated, and therefore off-brand, experience. If you're training customers to ignore your prime real estate, it has lost its value. There are places I won't go into because they are so run down that they look like they're closed for business. A welcoming physical environment attracts people; it's part of a positive on-brand experience.

For example, I usually stay away from all-you-can-eat sushi restaurants. My own perception is that they serve lower-quality sushi. I live near two sushi restaurants, one all-you-can-eat. At one of the sushi restaurants, my regular haunt, the staff knows my name. One night it was closed, but the friend I was with knew of another sushi pace: the all-you-can-eat place. The front of the building looked dated, dark, and uninviting. It hasn't changed in the thirteen years I've lived here. No glass windows so you couldn't see inside; it's all dark paneling, with a door and a sign that says "All You Can Eat Sushi." My curbside appraisal was "Run-down, probably poor quality." Had I been alone, I would have skipped sushi that night. But it was the only open sushi in town and I agreed to go. When we walked through the door, I was surprised. It was lovely! It was clean, well set up, and filled with people eating: things you miss from the street with no windows or glass front. Think how much business companies miss from people who look at them and say, "No thanks." People are evaluating you even before they come in, not just physically but by reading reviews. Are you creating the value that invites them in? Are your touchpoints, all your points of customer contact, on-brand or off-brand for your business?

SEEING YOUR BUSINESS THROUGH YOUR CUSTOMERS' EYES

Not being aware of your customers often leads to off-brand experiences. We've all seen them: a team member eating at the cash register; ballpoint pens lying open on a counter near white clothing; side conversations among team members that ignore or exclude customers; not being open when hours are clearly posted on the door, or not posting a reason why your business is closed. All these small acts add up to customers' distrust.

You can, however, change an unwelcoming environment. If you consciously design a front-stage, on-brand experience in your store, you direct how people interact and respond to it. And that can quickly change how people perceive your unique value.

Part of your awareness when designing your front-stage, on-brand business is capturing customer feedback in the form of surveys, conversations, emails, and a suggestion box.

Because this awareness is so important, I created a tool to make it easier for owners and teams to identify the customer experience they're creating in all the different parts of their business. It's called The Touchpoint Scorecard™. It's a tool to raise your knowledge of the customer experience by asking you to be the customer and rate different aspects of your business as a customer would at all points of contact. It even identifies those touchpoints.

For instance, you can consider the physical environment (*Are your Christmas lights still up in February?*); your printed material, including brochures, invoices, and business cards; and your receipts. These are all opportunities to enhance the customer's experience and reinforce your value. It works to build team awareness, which helps team members be more efficient, make solid decisions, and make changes to constantly improve the business. It opens your eyes wide enough to see your business through customers' eyes.

Other touchpoints include the types of interactions we've mentioned earlier: how team members answer the phone, welcome guests to the store, answer questions, handle the payment process, etc. Then, there is technology: all the different ways we connect electronically via websites, smartphones, voicemail, email, social media, text, and still, occasionally, fax. Can customers reach you easily? How long does it take you to answer emails? How else can they reach you? How functional is your website? Do you have a phone tree? Does the customer feel a sense of connection and efficiency dealing with you, or is the process cumbersome? Do your actions or policies create added value, or are they a barrier? The idea is to identify all the points of contact in *your* business, and then you rate yourself in each area, from one to ten, as though you were a customer.

Retail Touchpoint Scorecard

Category	Touchpoint	Worst Experience 1	2	3	4	5	6	7	8	9	Best Experience 10
Print	ads (newspaper, direct mail)										
	brochures										
	informational sheets										
	receipt										
Human	telephone reception										
	initial entering of store										
	customer questions										
	locating products										
	'trying out' product										
	cashier/check out										
	floor staff										
Physical	appearance of store										
	products and displays										
	ease of finding desired items										
	appearance of staff										
Technology	website										
	phone system/voicemail										
	email										
	fax										
	database										
Overall Customer Experience		1	2	3	4	5	6	7	8	9	10

Click here: www.TouchPointScorecardTraining.com for FREE training on how to use this valuable tool!

> To download your copy of The TouchPoint Scorecard along with support to get the most out of using it, go to www.TouchPointScorecardTraining.com.

The self-assessment is intended to build team awareness. It's an awareness checklist that identifies new opportunities to increase connection and value for customers. Identify one or two touchpoints at a time and brainstorm with your team how to improve the experience you are creating.

> ## BRANDING WITH RECEIPTS
>
> Do you know that your receipts are a customer touchpoint? Because we rarely think about them, they are underutilized as an on-brand tool. Yet, that's what your customers leave with as a record of their experience with you that day. A well-designed logo on a store receipt reinforces your company's value. It needs to be complete with a description of the purchase, the cost, the date, the return policy, and a thank you. Care with your receipt's design and information reinforces customers' sense of feeling connected and being taken care of, as does being asked where they want the receipt, in the bag or in their hand. Don't forget your receipt!

I've found that this process has two direct advantages for independent businesses. First, it creates a much wider awareness of all your touchpoints with customers. Second, it bridges the gap between your vision and their actual experience. It can be amazing to discover what customers notice and what affects them—details of which the owner and team members are often not aware. For example, a nail salon that I know of found that having its televisions set to news channels made clients anxious, and they were there to relax. I'm noticing that its TVs now are tuned to cooking shows.

Using a touchpoint scorecard lets you identify simple changes that create an experience that builds trust and relationship with your customers—and enhances and supports the value of your business.

Combining the front-stage/back-stage and on-brand/off-brand models with the touchpoint scorecard gives you the tools to train your team. It also creates the *alignment* that every business needs to stay consistent in those two models, play its own game of business, and avoid being commoditized. It becomes an integrated part of how you operate. Total customer focus and experience doesn't end with checking off items on the scorecard. To keep your success ongoing, you must also have regular communication that reinforces that. That includes regular team reviews of the customer touchpoints experience. Customer awareness must always be front and center in your business; it must be continually talked about.

The best way to do this is to have a regular meeting structure in place. It doesn't matter how many employees you have. Even if you have a team of three, you still need to have regular meetings. Someone might say, "But we talk all the time!" Yes, but regular team meetings focus on the touchpoints and how the team will apply data and knowledge to improve them. You want to ensure that what you talk about will make a difference!

We'll cover this more in the next chapter. The goal is to provide value not only in the services you deliver to individual customers but to enhance their experience of doing business with you. Actions as small as moving scented products away from the door to avoid triggering some customers' scent sensitivity, changing your endcaps, and placing displays safely out of the way cost nothing for the business to implement but result in customers feeling valued. When customers have a consistent front-stage, on-brand experience with your business, they feel taken care of, they feel connected, and they feel like they have a relationship with you. Every interaction that a customer has with you creates an experience, that creates an impression, that creates a relationship. Positive experiences are the building blocks that make customers feel related, appreciated, and connected to you.

> Every interaction that a customer has with you creates an experience, that creates an impression, that creates a relationship.

How to keep that relationship positive and moving forward means ongoing team give and take. The first step is designing it, the second step is maintaining it and having it be consistent. That's what we'll talk about in the next chapter.

CHAPTER SEVEN

TEAM ENGAGEMENT AND TRAINING

One recent Christmas, I went to a clothing store to buy a $100 gift card for a friend. I knew she loved the brand, so I was happy when I entered the store. When I bought the card, the clerk at the register was friendly. But as soon as she closed her register, she turned her back on me and started talking to the other clerk about a concert they'd attended. I was still standing in front of her at the counter, closing my wallet and putting it back in my purse. I felt dismissed. Why?

Until a customer leaves the counter, you're not done!

Her message was very clear: the store had my money and didn't need anything else from me. I was a *transaction*, not a *person*.

If the clothing store had trained employees to pay attention to the customer experience, I would have left feeling as happy as when I'd arrived. The cashier had been pleasant to me during the transaction, but her awareness vanished when her perceived part was done. Nobody wants to be seen as a wallet.

The store missed an opportunity to turn me into a fan, never mind a raving fan.

This is one way a team that is not aware of the customer experience hurts independent businesses. It loses customers who feel unseen and unheard. The business loses revenue. And, it loses—or doesn't build—perceived value to customers.

It is up to the owner to build and train a vibrant, *engaged* team.

Why is this so important?

It is important—absolutely necessary, in fact—because team members are the people who interact with customers day-to-day. If they don't understand what the business really offers—why customers should choose your business—they are not playing your game of business. If they don't know what the owner's goals are, or if they're not on board with them, the result is frustrated customers (and team members). Your team is the delivery mechanism of either success or failure. Team engagement is critical to building relationships with customers that keep them coming back—and raving about your business to others.

This is true with any business of any size. The entrepreneur *relies* on the team to engage with customers. So, if the entrepreneur is not clear what the business is, or the values it creates, team members have no GPS to position the business for success and keep it moving in that direction. They may be paying attention to what they sell, but they also need to understand the impact they have on customers and the entire business.

As your brand ambassadors, all team members must be in the communication loop. That includes those who may not be on the front stage but who provide valuable support to those who are. Back-stage marketing people, stock handlers, technicians, mailroom clerks, order entry, HR and accounting are all key to delivering your value to customers. If communication gaps from owner to team members or among the team itself are causing mistakes and customer frustration, they are costing you business. The owner sets customer expectations; the team has to deliver on them.

Full team engagement results in increased energy and productivity, less turnover, and a better workplace culture. Who wouldn't want to work in a business that makes them feel like they're having an impact in their community? They are proud of what they do and where they work. Consider that if your team is your main delivery system for creating on-brand experiences with your customer, your perception shifts from payroll being one of your biggest expenses to one of your biggest assets—if you have an engaged team.

> Full team engagement results in increased energy and productivity, less turnover, and a better workplace culture.

For this to happen, the team needs to be set up to win.

SETTING UP A WINNING TEAM

All employees want to feel like they are winning in their job. When no one has laid out clear expectations, tasks, and standards, it's not apparent to team members how to do that. They spend much of their time guessing. And when people guess, often they operate from fear and control. That has an impact on their productivity. If they spend time guessing at their jobs, they're not spending time doing what they should in their role. Setting clear expectations takes the guesswork out of winning.

There are four key components to setting up a team to win.

The first is training team members to know the clear value proposition of the business. Everyone on the team must fully understand what the business really provides. It's not enough to say, "Solutions." This step calls for specificity; why is their workplace unique and special to customers? Team members must be able to answer that to deliver value to customers. They must feel like experts in their role, driven by purpose. This goes back to Daniel Pink's finding in his book, *Drive: The Surprising Truth About What Motivates Us*, that workers today most want to feel a sense of *purpose*.

This idea upends the conventional wisdom about what motivates people to work. It isn't primarily external drivers like money and incentive programs. It's internal drivers: the deeply human need to direct our own lives, to learn and create new things, and to do better by ourselves in our world. We want what we do to *matter*. That gives us greater autonomy and motivates us to contribute more.

A business that gives its team members a clear sense of purpose has the answers to three questions—and every team member must know them. They are:

1. What value does your business provide?

2. Why do customers choose you—and keep coming back?

3. What do your customers say?

The second component to setting up a team to win is having a clear position agreement for every team member. This goes beyond a job description that defines the *responsibilities* of the role. A position agreement takes that to the next level, specifically answering, "What are the *standards for being successful* in that role?" For instance, if store clerks are responsible for welcoming customers as they come through the door, the standard might be that customers are *greeted within three steps of being in the store.* Every job task and responsibility you assign to a team member should carry with it specified standards and expectations. How are they a part of creating solutions-based, on-brand experiences.

The third component to winning is regular team communication. The most successful independent companies I work with have structured times and agendas; at the bare minimum, fifteen- to twenty-minute weekly huddles for those in the same role, and full team meetings at least monthly. They should start on time and end on time.

Owners often tell me when I first meet them, "Oh, I talk to my team members all the time." They mean on an informal, "I-ran-into-Joe-in-the-break-room" basis. That's not good enough; you need *regular, planned* communication.

A simple meeting structure would be: everyone shares the results they produced last week; discusses current projects, with the owner sharing information about them that the team needs to know; and sets commitments to report on the following week. Of course, work teams vary with shifts, flex-time, part-time, and full-time workers, so tailor your meetings accordingly. Regularity is the most important aspect of team communication; it reminds team members that they're a key part of the business and keeps everyone up to speed. Nothing says, "You matter" like sharing face-to-face.

Regular communication should be a core value for businesses of every size, but independent owners often let it go because they think they *are* communicating with their team. And they may be talking to them, but what they're not doing is creating a *structure* that assures team members that they are in the communications loop. The information flow has to be two-way. Structured communication is important; without it, team members spend their time guessing what the owner wants and don't experience their role as part of something bigger than their tasks. They should know *why* they matter.

And it's not just top-down communication that's important; the team needs a vehicle for communication amongst themselves too. Bob Lomenick, owner of Tyson Drug in Holly Springs, Mississippi, identified a communication disconnect with his team. Like many owners of multiple stores, he realized that he often talked to the different teams informally but didn't necessarily share the same information consistently. With no regular cross-team communication structure, his people were often guessing what to do and how to win. He saw the impact of confusion in team productivity and customer service.

So, Bob developed a two-pronged strategy for internal communication. The first was that each store team have a regular weekly huddle and a monthly all-team meeting.

His second idea was to create a message board that could be shared among his stores. All team members had access to it, both for posting and reading messages. They were trained to consult the message board regularly and always at the start of a shift. They use it for everything from locating customers' prescriptions to announcing shift schedules.

Bob shared with me the story of a customer who'd come in to pick up a prescription. The technician she'd spoken to on the phone happened to be at lunch and the technician on duty couldn't find the prescription. He went to the message board and, *voila*, there was a message from the first technician with information for the customer, should the customer get there during the lunch break. The relief technician was able to help the customer—who, in turn, felt taken care of. A far better outcome than in most stores, where unlucky timing usually elicits the answer, "He's out. I don't know what to tell you."

Remarkably, Bob noticed that as soon as he devised a regular communication structure, the team's cohesiveness changed dramatically. Working together to support one another, Bob's team members stay focused on Tyson Drug's unique value proposition (We manage your medications so you can manage your life—our mission is to help our patients live longer, healthier lives); realize the impact that they, as individuals, have on the team and on customers; and focus on the results they produce.

CASE STUDY: BOB LOMENICK WITH TYSON DRUGS IN HOLLY SPRINGS, MS

Independent pharmacy owners have been facing radically reduced reimbursement rates over the last ten years to the point that, without careful attention, 20 percent or more of the prescriptions they are filling are less than their purchase price (and that doesn't include operating and dispensing costs). Plus, it's estimated that 30 to 50 percent of patients are noncompliant to their prescribed medications and Bob's team were constantly dealing with issues from patients not taking their meds correctly.[16]

What would be an UpSolution? Bob heard an idea of synchronizing a patient's medications, so they are filled together once a month, while at an industry conference. He saw the potential both to streamline his internal processes and make it much easier for patients to take their medication as prescribed. He created the Tyson Drugs Ready Med Program. The outcome was better patient adherence, better patient outcomes (sometimes leading to reducing or eliminating some of their meds), streamlined inventory

---

16 Fred Kleinsinger, "The Unmet Challenge of Medication Nonadherance," *The Permanente Journal*, https://www.ncbi.nlm.nih.gov/pmc/articles/PMC6045499/.

> and fill time, and the ability to become a central role for patients in making their life easier and helping them manage their meds and health.

When setting up regular team communication, what you're doing is *investing* in your team. By investing time to create and utilize a regular communication structure, you increase team productivity and engagement. That sets up the team to win.

I have found some owners are reluctant to structure communication. They say things like, "I talk to them anyway, why does it have to be scheduled?" (So everyone hears the same thing at once.) "Meetings are a waste of time." (Not if they're focused.) "We're too busy for that." (Not all the time—spend 15 minutes now to save hours later.)

This is where you can be adaptive. For some stores, a fifteen-minute huddle before opening is a good start to each day. My friends, Len and Annette, who have the carpet cleaning and restoration business, do this. At 8:00 a.m. sharp, before team members go out into the field, they discuss what happened the day before, what they need to know that day, and what the priorities are. Your group huddle may not have to be every day; once a week may be a better fit. Then post the notes from the meeting where team members can easily access them. That helps both those who missed the meeting and those who want a memory refresh.

It's important to have a structure in place so your team knows *when* the communication is happening. Ideally, it's at the same time each week. When there is a rhythm, team members know what to expect and can prepare to listen and share.

The moment structured communication is put in place as an operating practice, it creates a better environment for a team to win.

Again, your team members are the ones delivering your business and your brand. If they're not in the information loop, they don't understand the goals or know the impact they have—or can have. They need to know what's working or not working for you *and* your customers. Then they can adjust.

The fourth component to setting up a team to win is to give all team members regular feedback so that they know how they're doing in their role. Often, companies have an annual review structure; I have found that the most successful independent companies share feedback with team members more often. For some, that means a quarterly review; the frequency doesn't matter as much as your awareness of providing specific feedback to team members on what's working and not working in their role. Along with regular feedback on their performance, it's important that this one-to-one communication lay out your clear expectations for their improvement and growth.

My method of providing feedback is to first communicate what's working and what's not working for a team member and then set clear expectations. Start with comments identifying what team members are doing that is positive. Be specific about what they are doing well in their role. Specificity is the key to good feedback.

For instance, "Jane, I just want to say thank you. I saw the interaction you had with Mrs. Smith. I saw that she was frustrated and you were present with her and really heard her and took care of her. And she left with a smile on her face. It was a pleasure to watch you take care of her. You really had an impact on her, which reflects on our business. You're good with customers, and always with a smile. I get so many positive comments back from customers about how much they enjoy working with you."

The same is true of communicating what isn't working, now

that the team member has receptive ears for corrective feedback. Be specific.

For example, "What's not working, Jane, is that, in the past month, you've been late to work five times. We schedule everyone on the team because they matter, they make a difference, and we have to be able to count on you. If you're not here, you're letting your team down. What do you find is the challenge to being on time? Let's brainstorm some strategies to correct that."

Finally, set clear expectations. "We expect you to be at your workstation when your shift starts. That means you'll probably have to come in the door five to ten minutes earlier so that you can take your coat off, get ready, maybe get a cup of coffee, and you're all set to go."

Not that it's always easy. I once had to communicate to a client account manager that if she was in a negative mood, she was like a black hole in the workshop room.

I could only have a corrective conversation that would be productive if I could start by acknowledging something she was doing well. I realized that she had the most powerful energy I'd ever experienced from someone. When she was "on," she created a wonderful, engaging space that drew people in, which is why she was so successful managing her accounts. But when she was off, it felt like she sucked the oxygen out of the room. When that happened, her coworkers didn't want to be around her. She had no idea how exhausting and negative she could be.

When I acknowledged her powerful energy, she beamed. Then I said, "This is what I've noticed. When you're on, this happens. And when you're off, this happens. And it impacts the results of the whole room."

We had a wonderful conversation! We talked about bringing her awareness of her powerful energy into the workshop room and staying conscious of what she was creating with it. We talked about how to have the team interact with her if something triggered a descent into the black hole. I believed she could change her behavior with conscious intent. And, if she couldn't, she wasn't the right person for that role. (She did and she was!)

The issue wasn't whether she was a fit for the team. She was actually a very good fit for the team. The issue was that she wasn't aware of the impact of her behavior on others.

When giving corrective feedback, you want to get someone's attention in a way that empowers and doesn't disengage them. By doing that, you create a structure to support team members so they can win in their job. Or, you might both learn that the job isn't the right fit for that person. I use a four-step corrective process: a verbal warning, a written warning, a final warning, and then, if there's no improvement, termination (or a move to a different role in the company that is a better fit).

The corrective action process is a key component of setting up the team to win. Team members need to know what their role is, the standards and expectations for the role, how they're doing in it, and the corrective action process, including the support they will get if they're not winning in their role.

I always want the entire corrective process to give the team member every possible chance to be able to hit the standards. But there also has to be an awareness that if they're not able to meet the standards, they can't continue in that role. There are three possible outcomes here: they begin to win in their job; they move to a different job; or they are no longer with the business.

Ideally, you want a continual feedback loop among all parties. The owner establishes the focus of the work environment and communicates it to the team members, who in turn communicate it to customers. Customers share their feedback on the experiences they've had. And then the team and owner discuss the feedback. This sets up continual improvement and shows where the business is not in alignment with customers' expectations. Then you can work to align them.

BRINGING ROLE PLAYING INTO THE EQUATION

One of my favorite team training tools is role playing. It's an excellent way to have your team fully appreciate the effect they have on customers. It emphasizes that setting up team members for success really depends on their awareness of the experience they're creating for customers (and each other). It's the least expensive and most powerful tool I've ever used for the team to understand the customer perspective.

Keep it simple and fun. Many people resist the exercise at first—the top reason for that is fear of embarrassment. To focus team members away from feeling uncomfortable to feeling empowered, I like to set up a bad case/good case scenario for common customer situations—simple ones, like how somebody answers the phone, or any action that gives customers their first impression of your business. Every interaction starts with a customer connection, whether it's on the phone or someone coming through the door.

So, ring-ring! "Hold the line, I'm busy. I'll get back to you." The team member role plays the customer. After he or she gets my brush off, I'll ask, "How do you feel?" The answer might be, "Annoyed. Or, this business doesn't care about me. I don't want to shop here."

Now, demonstrate the interaction as an attentive team member: Ring-ring! "Good morning, [name of business], how can I help you?" Then ask your "customer" how he or she feels. "I felt welcome, I felt appreciated, I want to shop here." Afterwards, have a follow-up discussion about how the team can use this awareness when interacting with customers.

The whole idea is for them to practice paying attention *to the customer's perspective and experience.* Earlier in this book, we discussed that team members often forget what it feels like to be on the customer side of the counter. This technique is a great way to show how you can bridge that gap.

Probably the most resistant team member to role play was … my own mother. She enlisted me to speak to a group of Sunday greeters that she belonged to at her church. Two designated greeters stationed themselves at the church doors each Sunday to welcome the worshippers. It was a warm and friendly congregation, with new members frequently joining. The greeters wanted to have regular members feel known and for new people checking out the church to feel welcomed.

It was a wonderful program that helped people new to the church feel accepted—they truly were brand ambassadors! My session with them was to, first, make them aware of the gap between an elder's perspective and a newcomer's perspective of the churchgoing experience. Then, I said, "What I'd like to do is role play here." Instant response from one of the group: "I hate role playing." That came from my mom. So, naturally I picked her. I had to; wouldn't you?

Thankfully, my mom is very gracious and accepted the challenge. (She was great.) We did a bad case/good case scenario. There were probably twenty or thirty people in the room watching. By re-creating "how-to" experiences, the group knew what it felt like to be the customer (or, in this case, the churchgoer).

You can see how every interaction—every relationship—depends on communication. I can't overstress that!

WHEN TO LET GO

One of the issues many business owners face is whether to keep a team member in a role simply because that person is good at the tasks involved. That doesn't mean he or she is a good fit on your team.

A retail environment, for instance, requires excellent people skills front stage. So, if a pharmacy technician is fast and accurate at counting pills but doesn't have good people skills—either with other team members or with customers—that's not a good fit. That team member needs a different job—or organization—to win.

In the book *Topgrading: The Proven Hiring and Promoting Method That Turbocharges Company Performance*, author and industrial psychologist Bradford D. Smart separates job candidates by designating them as "A," "B," and "C" players based on their skill sets for various jobs and the level of management they will likely need. "A" players have the right skill set for the job and need no or minimal management. "B" players have the skill set but need to be managed to produce excellent results. "C" players are disengaged—either they lack the necessary skill set for the job or don't have the right attitude for a good fit. Interestingly, Smart observes, "A" players will not stay long in an environment with "C" players.[17]

The owner is responsible for creating the environment and

---

17   Bradford D. Smart, *Topgrading: The Proven Hiring and Promoting Method That Turbocharges Company Performance,* 3rd ed. (New York: The Penguin Group, 2012).

culture that help team members engage to win. It is an ongoing, dynamic process. But if you have people on your team who never seem to be in alignment with the business or are unable to create consistent customer experiences, then you must look at what they're contributing to the team. They may be on the wrong seat in the right bus—their skills are valuable elsewhere in the business—or they may be on the wrong bus. In which case, you need to let them off.

Every business owner I've worked with has a story about finally letting go of a team member who wasn't a right fit and brought the team down. And then when that person left the company, the culture shifted dramatically—for the better—for the rest of the team.

A friend of mine who owns a marketing business, for instance, had a salesperson who brought in big accounts. She was good, no question. But she was also caustic, so caustic that she caused a lot of team turnover, not to mention stress. No one enjoyed working with her. She'd miss details. She'd miss meetings. She would fail to communicate with her team members. They would gladly tell you that she was a nightmare to work with. But she kept her job because she was bringing in sales.

At what cost though? When she finally left—the owner realized what was causing the turnover—the team experienced an immediate surge in energy. He found another salesperson who was the right fit for the company, a talent he couldn't find while holding on to a wrong fit. People now wanted to stay there.

When team members are unaware of how they affect the customer experience, they tend to focus on their *task* of the job or role rather than the *experience* they're creating. A good example are people hired to stock shelves in a grocery store. They may think their job is stocking shelves, but if they're doing it while customers are in the store, then their job is customer *service*. Unless they're stocking the shelves when the store is closed, they're in the front stage of the business. Stocking the shelves front stage and on brand would be paying attention to people who look lost and offering to help them find something. Or being available to ask questions. The off-brand way of stocking shelves, conversely, would be to keep your back to people so they don't ask you questions, or avoid eye contact, or any of the ways we shrink from unwanted interactions.

We can look again to Disney for another example of top team front-stage, on-brand engagement with customers.

Who would you expect to be the park's most important ambassadors?

If you guessed that it is the costumed characters or the train driver who chugs you around the park, you'd be wrong. It's the janitorial staff. It's the people who seem to appear out of nowhere with brooms and brushes two nanoseconds after your child's ice cream cone slips through her fingers and splats on the ground. One to clean up the spill and one with a replacement cone. These uniformed brand ambassadors are the eyes and ears of the customer experience and the cast members guests approach with questions.

It's important to reinforce with communication what you want from team members. Chances are that yours are not as ever-present as Disney's cleanup crew, but they do share the vision of stepping in to help someone out. And that presents another opportunity to give individual feedback and, especially, praise. When the focus is on their positive actions, team members show their engagement.

Innovative pharmacy owner Chris Cornelison created a culture of excellence by devising a simple structure to reinforce the value of customer care in his stores. His structure included making it easy to remember and follow. His recognition program uses poker chips. He starts every day with five poker chips in his left pocket. His goal for himself—and he also encourages his managers to do the same—is to find five things to acknowledge team members for over the course of the day. Each time he does that, he moves a poker chip from his left pocket to his right. If he sees more than five, the chips switch pockets again, one at a time.

Many independent business owners have good intentions to acknowledge team members the way Chris does, but if you don't have a structure, the feedback won't happen regularly. What is a recognition structure that will work for you? Your team members will love you for it and it will be a constant reminder to them that their role is to be a brand ambassador, no matter what their job.

As your brand ambassadors, they create the experience of your business. Give them the best environment to do that in. To recap:

- Always set up your team to win by being clear on your business's value proposition and training the team to deliver it.

- Have agreements for each position so the team member who fills it knows the standards for the role.

- Regular, structured communication is key.

- So is regular feedback.

With all this in place, your team is set up to win. Your culture of engagement makes your business a place where people want to work. And, you create the relationships and solutions with your customers that make you stand out as winners in your game of business.

RECOGNIZE AND REWARD

A rule of thumb is that whatever you put your attention on is what expands, so setting team members up to win includes acknowledging and rewarding their success. Team member recognition is a key operating practice. Recognize team members' progress in your regular team meetings.

Who isn't proud to see their name and picture featured as "Employee of the Week" (or whatever your internal recognition program is)? Best of all, structured individual feedback keeps "right fit" team members on track and protects the culture you've created for your business.

CHAPTER EIGHT

THE NEED FOR CONTINUOUS EVOLUTION

When I buy TVs or other electronic equipment I don't know much about, I rely on in-store customer service. Or at least I hope to. What I have found is that most of the national chain stores aren't very good at helping customers make buying decisions. Like my friend Dan with the shelves, I can eventually find the right aisle for what I'm after. But, unlike Dan's experience, I often find that the national chains' team members have little or no expertise in the store's specific items or brands. Most haven't been trained to ask me the questions that would reveal my specific needs. I've had to invent my own learning process. So, I try to educate myself based on the scant information that team members can tell me, internet searches, and by asking friends everything from how to mount a wall TV to what LED technology is.

I have wished it was *easier* for me to make my buying decision—

and feel confident that it was right for me. Nobody willingly chooses the frustration and disappointment of finding out that something you bought doesn't work for you. Nobody is happy going back to the store to wait on the customer returns line. We'd all prefer to go to one place where team members ask you questions like, "What size room will your TV go in?" "What do you like to watch on TV?" (because, apparently, there's a big difference between watching sports or drama), and "How close to the screen do you want to be?"

I ended up buying a flat-screen LED TV when the technology was new only because I finally went into an independent electronics store. I thought I'd spend about $400 and wanted a flat screen to replace my old bulky TV. A knowledgeable team member in that store explained that an LED screen uses less electricity and lasts longer than plasma and LCD technology. I spent $1,200 on a TV—three times more than I'd planned. And, I was *happy with my purchase*. The team member listened to me and solved my issues before I even knew what they were. He offered me an UpSolution.

UpSolutions keep us "up" on the flow of innovation! Continuous innovation leads to our continuous evolution.

Independent businesses must plan for continuous evolution. Nothing about your business is fixed, including the technology, the products and services, or even whether it operates in a bricks-and-mortar space. Innovation expands customer needs and wants; possibilities become solutions. You will always be poised for success if you are positioned to innovate.

Your ability to keep evolving requires constant awareness of five factors:

1. You must stay top of mind among your customers.
2. If you listen, your customers will always tell you what's next. Solving your customers' issues creates never-ending opportunity for your business.
3. Product innovation means continuous improvement.
4. Adaptability is a skill to be practiced and trained.
5. Complacency of current products and services is a recipe for disaster.

Let's examine each of these factors.

YOU MUST STAY TOP OF MIND AMONG YOUR CUSTOMERS

Staying top of mind among your customers means staying current in their thinking and planning. Generally, people only remember what they've been exposed to in the past month. That's a short window to keep their attention. This is why continuously changing and updating your visuals is so important—what's in your windows, your endcaps, and other elements of your front stage. When things have been up for too long, you are training your customers to ignore your prime display real estate.

Even when you have banked brand loyalty with your target customers over a period of time, take nothing for granted. You must sustain your brand's freshness—and your outreach to customers. Even the top brands in the world, the ones with instantly recognizable logos, must do this. For example, Apple, the best-known brand in the world according to the *Forbes* 2018 Most Valuable Brand list, continually develops new products and new product models. When the company introduced its iPhone X in 2017, it was the first iPhone with an OLED display. Less than a year later, Apple debuted its iPhone XS and XS Max. Continual evolution has meant improved video and camera capabilities, facial recognition, faster performance, new screen sizes, and longer battery life.

Independent companies must see their unique opportunities to evolve their solutions and services too. The only difference between your evolutionary process and that of the classic big brands is *scale*. The premise is the same: innovate or stagnate.

Guinness is one of the best-known brands in Ireland—it's been brewed there since 1759. (Today, it's also brewed in almost fifty countries and sold in 150.) If any company could rest on its laurels, it's Guinness. But Guinness knows that it can't do that and continue to thrive. The company still continually advertises and has a history—and culture—of innovation. In 1959, the company launched its Guinness Draught product, the first beer produced with nitrogen, not carbon dioxide. That started an industry trend that is alive and well today as craft brewers improve nitro beers. And in 2016, Guinness tackled a shift in customer preferences, using a new filtration process to make its products vegan.[18]

Which leads us to the second premise of continuous evolution: *If you listen, your customers will always tell you what's next. Solving your customers' issues creates never-ending opportunity for your business.*

This is why I advocate engaged listening to what your customers are telling you about your business. And why you should *always* listen, even—especially—when they are complaining, however loudly or angrily. (And it often doesn't get to that point if your team

---

18   Simon Thomsen, "Guinness is changing its recipe to become vegan friendly," *Business Insider*, November 4, 2015, https://www.businessinsider.com/guinness-is-changing-its-recipe-to-become-vegan-friendly-2015-11.

is trained to be fully aware of the customer experience.) They are not only telling you what's wrong (or right!), they are also always telling you what's *next*. Listen for new opportunities to serve them in every interaction.

Sometimes it's helpful to check in with yourself to test whether you really have been listening and learning. For instance, questions you might want to ask—and answer— are: Knowing what you know now, would you still make that decision? (All credit to business author Peter Drucker for that one.) Has there been a shift in customers, the team, the market, or technology that creates an opportunity to modify or develop new UpSolutions for your target customers? Should you introduce or discontinue some feature of your business?

Your customers have the answers.

Sometimes the answer isn't what it appears to be, or brings with it an unexpected outcome. For example, an independent women's retail business I know consolidated its two bricks-and-mortar stores into a single location when the lease on one ran out. The owner took that opportunity to scale down the business to have more time with her family. But the two stores attracted slightly different demographics, and her team quickly found that even the most loyal clients of the closed store were unhappy with the change of location. They told team members that they were sad and disappointed they'd lost "their" store. They complained that they now had to drive an extra distance (about five miles) and had to pay for street parking (the other store had a free parking lot); there was no children's section or sale room; and there was no plus-size section.

The owner and team shared what customers were telling them and considered their needs. They knew they couldn't accommodate every concern. The other store *was* five miles away and the one that stayed open was under a long-term lease. The metered street parking was the city's doing. The store was smaller than the closed one—there was simply no room for a children's section or sale room. So, the owner looked at the opportunity voiced by customers that they *could* make work. She stocked fewer housewares and used the freed-up space to put in a special rack for plus-size customers.

Then came the unexpected outcome. The reality was that although some customers had really wanted the plus-size clothing choices, the rack did not rack up *enough* sales to sell inventory off quickly or serve enough customers in the new location to have a significant impact on the bottom line. And, established customers missed the variety in housewares.

The owner asked herself, "Knowing what I know now, would I still make that decision?" And the answer was: No! Her decision was based on the best information she had at the time from her most trusted advisors—her customers. But that information needed the context of a bigger picture—in this case, the percentage of overall sales that the new rack would account for—to clarify that this solution for customers wasn't working for her, the business owner.

The need for clothes that fit *all* her customers properly was still there, though. So, she devised an innovation for everybody. The store continues to carry plus-size clothing. Every customer can now find her size on the store's racks, where a full range of sizes are integrated. A larger selection of housewares is now back on the floor. And while there was no space for a sale room, there is now a designated sale rack.

When you're listening to what your customers are asking and telling you—and using that information to solve their needs—you can't help but continuously evolve. They provide the information that answers the question, "Knowing what you know now, would you make the same decision?"

Business owners and team members make the best decisions based on that they know at the time. The issue is that often the decision is not revisited later based on what they've learned since. I like to remind teams that evolution is a process, not an event. So, while you may have made changes to reflect customer needs and wants at one time, you're not done. Everything changes; retail, especially, is in a perpetual state of flux. And if you do implement something based on customer feedback, but your good business intentions turn out to be the wrong fit, then the moment you know that, get out! There is no point in dragging out a losing experiment. Instead identify what you learned and focus on what makes your business unique and your UpSolutions truly helpful.

One thing independent companies can do to gather information from a representative group of customers at one time is to form customer advisory groups. The business owner can meet with them occasionally to give the whole team feedback and to test new ideas. You want their perspective: What's working? What's not working? Do they have any improvement ideas? Any suggestions?

If you do ask people in the community to be part of a feedback or discussion group, then do something special for participants. Take care of them as they take care of you. That could mean taking them out for a nice dinner as a group or giving each of them a special gift. Acknowledge, in some way, the importance of their insight and feedback as well as their time and participation. Listen. Pay attention. Learn. And then use customers' feedback to continuously evolve.

PRODUCT INNOVATION MEANS CONTINUOUS IMPROVEMENT

The main way to see how product innovation is connected to continuous improvement is simply to pay attention to what does and doesn't work. Then, keep doing what works and *change what doesn't*. If that sounds simple, consider this: changing what doesn't work is an ongoing process. If you don't always have a place in your business to put an imaginary "Under Construction" sign, you're not aware of everything happening in your store and with your customers. I don't want to suggest that there's no wisdom in the old saying, "If it ain't broke, don't fix it." I do want to stress the importance of doing course corrections *before* anything breaks. That means taking a proactive approach—innovating whenever and wherever you see an opportunity.

Earl Nightingale comes to mind. Sometimes called "The Dean of Personal Development," Nightingale was a radio broadcaster and motivational speaker who was inspired by the legendary 1937 book *Think and Grow Rich* by Napoleon Hill. He embraced these words of Hill's: "We become what we think about." Nightingale wrote his own motivational book, *The Strangest Secret,* that also became one of the all-time great business books.[19]

An early leader of the personal awareness movement, Nightingale advocated continuous improvement in business and life. Building on Hill's premise that "We become what we think about," he believed that every business must be continuously undergoing improvement. Continuous improvement creates forward momentum for the team and an always-renewed and renewable sense of purpose. If remodeling your entire house seems overwhelming and unaffordable, you can renovate one room at a time. The point is, don't wait for conditions to be perfect to improve your business or your life. Conditions will

---

19   Earl Nightingale, *The Strangest Secret* (Naperville, Illinois: Simple Truths, 1957).

never be perfect. Yet, there is *always* something to do that will move you forward.

For instance, refresh those endcaps, signs, and windows regularly. Train team members to be knowledgeable about new products and services. Rotate what's on sale weekly or biweekly.

Imagine a business where nothing is status quo. A business is either growing or dying, like grass. We become what we think about. When you think of improvements to your business, your business improves. And growth does not always mean getting bigger; it's not everyone's dream to grow a company and take it public. When you play your own game of business, growth can be anything you want it to be. Improvement is growth. Innovation is growth. Repositioning leads to growth.

I once had a client in the packaging business who was feeling squeezed by marketplace changes. They were struggling to maintain their revenue and their profit margin was shrinking. They were being forced to compete for jobs through a Request for Proposal process (FRP) that led to continually lowering the pricing of jobs to get a contract.

What the owners wanted was to stay in business, reverse their profit trend, and continue to serve their customers with their unique value proposition. Only, in the face of dramatic market changes, the positioning of what they had to offer needed to change.

They'd grown a successful business as a packaging house, but that was before RFPs had created a bidding war. What was their unique value proposition now?

To answer that question, they surveyed their customers to see how *their* needs were (or weren't) now being met and what they appreciated working with the packaging company.

My client was surprised to discover that their "best fit" customers had changed. While customers had once looked to his business to create unique packaging, they now focused on finding complete and seamless integrated solutions for packaging *and* delivery. Their new "best fit" customers were in consumer-packaged goods.

The team completely repositioned to offer services from package design to fulfillment and became an integrated retail expert with their customers, moving up the delivery chain to contribute to the initial package design when their customers were launching new consumer-packaged goods. The company now provided an end-to-end solution for customers. The result: a 35 percent increase in revenue that first year. And profits doubled.

There is always a clear line that connects product innovation and continuous improvement. Listening to your customers can't help but inspire you to innovate. Don't miss the opportunities for growth, for becoming what you—and your customers—think about.

ADAPTABILITY IS A SKILL TO BE PRACTICED AND TRAINED

Continuous evolution also means continuous adaptability. The willingness to adapt is only one element of this premise; adaptability is a skill that, like all skills, must be practiced. This is a key part of team training and empowerment. If team members are trained only to repeat a rigid policy of saying "No" to a customer, you are guaranteed angry customers who probably won't be coming back. An independent business can't afford *not* to adapt to change.

A great example of that is Aran Sweater Market, a small company with a global reach from its home on the Aran Islands, just off Ireland's west coast. It's a great example of how a team used the skill of adaptability to extend the reach of a local company in a remote place to worldwide recognition.

Using the wool of Aran's famous sheep, islanders had the start of a knitting industry by the end of the nineteenth century. Aran sweaters have complex, intricately textured stitches, which made them famous in Ireland and among visitors there. When they were shown in *Vogue* magazine in 1956, the world took notice. As exports grew, Aran's knitters remained true to their island home. They also stayed true to their original product. But they knew they had to adapt to changes in the global economy to stay viable and vibrant as a business. They used the internet and social media to showcase the sweaters and share their history. You can like them on Facebook, pin them on Pinterest, and order them on Amazon. Aran Sweaters came up with a brilliant innovation to expand Aran Sweater's global reach: if you have an Irish name, or know someone who does, there is a specific stitch pattern for each of the five hundred-plus Irish clan names in the knitters' database. I know; I ordered two of them.

Aran's practice of adaptability and training its team to use it for positive change led it to become a brand icon in Ireland and fueled global demand. It is key to any company's continuous evolution.

What happens when you realize changes that require adaptability—but you don't want to go in that direction?

One option is moving on to a new venture. I think of the pharmacy owner I knew who sold his store because he didn't want to adapt to the market and demographic changes that were trending. He was no longer excited about the business. And, good for him—if you think it's time to sell, don't wait: if sales trend downward, your business will lose market value. Continuous evolution requires both adaptability and enthusiasm from every member of the team. And to that pharmacy owner, congratulations for building a business that someone wanted to buy!

COMPLACENCY OF CURRENT PRODUCTS AND SERVICES IS A RECIPE FOR DISASTER

Continuous improvement—and thus, evolution—is not comfortable. But complacency is not an option for independent businesses. Think of the status quo as the "static quo." Being willing to learn, grow, and question—and then innovate—is the only way forward. Business books are filled with examples of big companies that went under when they remained complacent in the face of changing technology or delivery models, including Kodak, Borders, and Blockbuster Video, to name just a few. Independent businesses with a fixed course are just as vulnerable.

If it were possible to stop change, we'd still have analog television, cars without seat belts or airbags, and Palm Pilots (remember them?). Independent businesses have unlimited opportunities to expand their products and services, their relationships with customers, and their unique value proposition—if they play their right game of business.

> **CASE STUDY: FARM TO PAW— BOUTIQUE AND MARKET**
>
> Owner Barb Spears chose to open a boutique pet retail store in a small town to service the surrounding areas. At a time when traditional brick and mortar stores seem to be struggling, she decided to open her business. Barb is a certified canine nutritionist and the boutique carries healthy pet food options, treats, and a range of accessories. They have offered classes including canine first aid. The store is a great example of creating a community around their business and knowing who their customers are. Barb and the Farm to Paw team are often found at local events with their dogs, and

they have built an active social media following. In a short period of time they have built a base of raving fans.

CONCLUSION

BRAVE NEW WORLD

Throughout this book, you've met independent business owners who successfully transformed their businesses in the face of price-based competition from online, national chain, and big-box stores. Today, those local businesses thrive, whether a pharmacy, bookstore, organic food market, motorcycle supply store, or carpet cleaning and maintenance business, among others. These diverse local enterprises have the common experience of innovating to play their own right game of business—and winning.

These owners are in the driver's seat for the road ahead. Their businesses will continue to flourish because they have successfully avoided being commoditized. They have not and will not be squeezed out of the market because, unlike the chain stores, they deliver *more* than transaction-based pricing. They deliver their own unique value by providing relationship-based solutions.

Change is a constant in every industry. The most successful independent businesses make sure that innovation and improvement are also constant. They will not be commoditized because they are clear on why customers choose them. They know what their customers need and want. They position themselves to showcase their value as a solution provider.

They also know how to effectively communicate that value. This is *how* they're winning at their own right game of business. And this is true for *any* independent business: the chains can't play *your* game of business! They can't. They offer the lowest perceived price. Transaction-based teams aren't trained to deliver solutions or build relationships. Independent businesses, on the other hand, win on value, solutions, and results. And, for them, creating UpSolutions is a game changer.

It takes the whole team to implement UpSolutions. Every team member gives and receives the professional information on which relationships—and customer solutions—are built. Unless the entrepreneur is the company's sole employee, it's the team that delivers the customer experience. It's the team members who work with customers on a day-to-day basis. For the business to succeed, all team members must have a clear understanding of the brand promise to know which solutions apply. They are the brand ambassadors. Brand ambassadors are poised to be heroes, and when they become heroes, customers become raving fans. When you help customers make an effective buying decision that solves their problems, you become their solution partner, creating greater value. Educating and offering solutions (the UpSolution recipe) empower customers to make the best decisions for them, and allow you to avoid competing based solely on price. You have to be seen to deliver the best value and results. And when the aligned customer experience builds rapport and trust, who would want to go anywhere else?

Why do UpSolutions work? Because when a team shifts its focus from *selling* to *helping customers make effective buying decisions*, your business empowers them not only to make their best choice but also to feel *good* about it. Being focused on your best fit customers puts you in the driver's seat for growth and change. And, it's a two-way street: customers share the information that tells you what they need, and team members share their wisdom and experience. Together, you build a partnership on trust, consistency, and dependability.

As we've discussed, a focused and consistent awareness of your customers is key to a company's success, if not its survival. That has always been true in business. But the market conditions for success have changed. For years, the majority of business was conducted locally; merchants knew everyone they served and everyone knew them. As our society expanded and became more urbanized, businesses moved to selling to people they didn't necessarily know. Scale brought a focus on sales transactions and efficiency. Now, as the internet drives global commerce and allows a company located anywhere to serve customers everywhere (like Aran Sweater Market), the rules of business have changed. The new business rules demand that businesses adopt a proactive attitude toward customer relationships rather than taking them for granted. Most of all, they demand wisdom—the wisdom of an owner's and team's experience—and consistently delivering an experience aligned with your brand's promise. Think of the motorcycle supply store owner who knew customers needed custom-fitted helmets to be as safe as possible on the road—and then provided them! The value he offered of a perfect fit outweighed the appeal of buying a cheaper helmet online.

Joe Polish, who founded Genius Network, which connects successful entrepreneurs, has said that customers will not buy from you unless you have both their trust and confidence. And for that, you have to be consistent. The moment you're not, you break that trust.

Just as in personal relationships, the core of professional relationships is trust.

When team members are set up for success, the trust they earn from customers generates revenue. Keeping that trust consistent means repeat business and customer retention, both of which are profit levers. On the back stage of the business, profit levers include an engaged team and team member retention.

This isn't to suggest that success for any business comes easily. In particular, the velocity of constant change in global business can seem daunting to independent owners. Some fear being left behind—for instance, they wonder, how can a small business keep up with every technology upgrade?

I see a larger business issue than software updates or new technology; to me, the question for owners to ask is, "What changes are my customers dealing with and how can I support them?" That is the core of continuous evolution—and continuous opportunities. By paying attention to trends and innovations specific to your customers and your industry, you can strategically plan how *you* can custom-fit new models in *your* business.

Independent businesses are often first to seize the day. In fact, the big players tend to hold on to their existing models or technology and often miss or delay the next disruptive technology. The digital camera was first invented at Kodak in 1975, but the manufacturer didn't bring it to market until late in the game because it chose to stay focused on selling film. The company that made the "Kodak Moment" famous became a business case study in missing the moment.

Independent businesses are freer to innovate and adapt trends to their own product or service niches. One interesting business trend that promises new opportunities is the subscription model. These are the meal kits, beauty boxes, and gift packages that regularly arrive at subscribers' doors, such as Bark Box for your dog, Causebox for the socially conscious, and enough "Geek" subscription boxes to merit numerous comparison websites. If a local independent business wanted to apply this model to its customers, say a boutique pet store that sells specialized dog food, the team could build a database of regular, "right fit" customers who value products personally selected for them according to their preferences (or their dog's) and provide additional value by delivering it right to their door. Delivery by drone and driverless vehicles is already happening in some places; everything, it seems, can show up at our homes. You can never go wrong by asking yourself how to make things easier for your customers.

Even before subscription boxes and Amazon Prime, network marketing companies had introduced auto-ship plans, where a single sale led to regular automatic shipments unless the customer acted to opt out. That was when simply *delivering* a product was no longer a sharp competitive edge. Now that the model is used to lock in customer retention, it's the quality of customer *contact* that affirms value in subscription and other delivery choices. Relationship-based businesses grow when customers know they *matter* to a business.

Transforming your business vision from a transaction-based model into the promise of unlimited value possibilities demands two mind-set shifts. The first is finding the opportunities in the challenges you face. The second is taking the actions that are needed to realize them. UpSolutions help you succeed at both.

The following points summarize this book—the secret ingredients of an UpSolution success story:

- *Know your two greatest assets* in devising UpSolutions: the information wellspring of your customers and the wisdom and experience of your team. Use UpSolutions to bridge the gap. Never underestimate the value of regular communication with either your customers or your team. Engage with all of them often.

- *Focus on always providing solutions for your customers* to clearly convey that your business is all about *them*. One independent hotel manager I know puts it this way: "The answer is yes. What was the question?"

- *Train your team to be brand ambassadors.* That will increase the perceived value your business provides to customers. No longer will the lowest advertised price be customers' purchase default setting. When brand ambassadors are heroes, customers become raving fans.

- *Build a front stage and a back stage* that align with and deliver your brand promise. Have clear parameters for what's *on-brand* and what's *off-brand.* Promote the former, correct the latter.

- *Align* both your value and the customer experience *with your brand promise.*

- *Adapt to market changes*, including emerging technologies, in a timely way based on shifting customer demographics and tastes. It's important to stay tuned to how customers' *own lives* are changing. Find the opportunity in the change.

- *Increase your value through continuous improvement and innovation*—and stay consistent—to positively impact two of your strongest profit leaders: repeat customers and team member retention.

UpSolutions was created in response to independent business owners and their teams who feel pressure to succeed in a market they're not designed to compete in. It is my passion to empower independent businesses. Why? Because independent businesses are the lifeblood of their communities. They're the engines in every community; they employ in their communities; they give back to their communities; they support and provide for their communities. For me, the UpSolution recipe was a way to empower them to differentiate themselves and feel like they're back in the driver's seat in their business. I firmly believe that if you know who your customers are—through observation, active listening, and probing questions—and position your business to create value for them—you have unlimited opportunities for growth.

To your success!

ABOUT THE AUTHOR

Patti Mara is the owner of Maranet Inc. and founder of The Profit Generator™, a program for business owners in retail and service-based industries to position their business for success and develop a loyal customer base. Patti enables business owners to navigate the changing marketplace and to understand and apply the "New Business Rules." This includes developing the ability to see their company from their customers' perspective and using the insights gained to consistently deliver "On Brand Customer Experiences," dramatically increasing customer retention, revenue, and profit.

A popular speaker, Patti has delivered breakthrough content to a variety of industries including financial services, home services, Women's Congress, commercial real estate, pharmacy owners, Entrepreneurs' Organization (EO), and restaurant owners.

Patti has over twenty-five years of experience designing and delivering customer service experiences and making the connection between customer experience and retention with the profit, results, and growth of a company.

Patti graduated from the University of Guelph with a bachelor of science degree and has furthered her studies by participating in and coaching leadership development and communication programs.

She is known for her abundant energy and her excellent rapport with clients and credits her connection with business owners to her understanding of the entrepreneurial spirit, her strong intuitive and communications skills, and her ability to effectively apply material to produce measurable business results.

For more information visit www.PattiMara.com.

ACKNOWLEDGMENTS

Northrup Frye in his book *An Educated Imagination* stated there is no such thing as original thought, we are all influenced by what we have learned and been exposed to.

This book is a culmination of ten years of thought and focus with many contributions and inspirations.

Many thanks to the clients and their teams I've had the privilege to work with. I greatly appreciate the trust and willingness to adapt and grow.

One of my pivotal relationships has been with Dan Sullivan and Babs Smith, the husband and wife team who founded and run Strategic Coach. Their brilliant insight helped me identify and focus on my unique ability and then expand my thinking to 10X and beyond. Thank you Dan and Babs, and the Strategic Coach team, for your encouragement and for creating this incredibly powerful, supportive community.

A special thank you to Shannon Waller who has been a sounding board and helped me formulate and organize my thinking into a book form.

A shout-out to all three of the powerful Waller women! Thank you Marilyn for your unyielding support and for connecting me with the right partner to finally make the book a reality.

In 2006 when I was ready to launch an online version of my Profit Generator Program, Joe Polish invited me to speak to his Platinum meeting in Phoenix. So many wonderful connections came out of that event, including carpet cleaning and restoration companies who were the first to go through the program. Many are friends to this day.

After that speech at Joe's event a gentleman came up to me and said, "You need to work with my industry." That man was Dan Benamoz. Thank you Dan for introducing me to your audience of independent pharmacy owners. What a privilege it has been to work with entrepreneurs who are so passionately committed to their communities.

And thank you Joe Polish! I've been introduced to so many incredible people and ideas through your connector powers!

Many thanks to the Eastwood family: Rick and Barb for being early champions and trusting me with your team and company; Andrea for your encouragement and early brainstorm sessions; and Rich and Bev for sharing your invaluable wisdom and experience. Talking with Rich felt like sitting with a master—cash flow first, then expenses and then sales.

To the community of entrepreneurs I am honored to be a part of—thank you! Special thanks to Kevin Thompson and Alex Nghiem for great positioning advice.

This book was an idea and an outline until I was connected to Advantage Media Group. Thank you to my publishing manager Elaine Best and my editorial manager Nate Best for guiding me through the process and pairing me with Pam Janis.

Pam, your role in the process was invaluable. You heard what I wanted to express, were excited at the content, and managed to

ACKNOWLEDGMENTS

capture my ideas in my voice. Thank you! Without you there would be no book.

And finally I'd like to thank my family. You are my rock! Special thanks to Wanda Mara for being my first reader and editor with outstanding advice.